T0193203

The Ultimate Scoring Drive

Defeating Eleven Barriers to a Victorious Life

DAVID B. WALL

WESTBOW
PRESS®
A DIVISION OF THOMAS NELSON
& ZONDERVAN

WestBow Press books may be ordered through booksellers or by contacting:

WestBow Press
A Division of Thomas Nelson & Zondervan
1663 Liberty Drive
Bloomington, IN 47403
www.westbowpress.com
1 (866) 928-1240

ISBN: 978-1-5127-0762-5 (sc)
ISBN: 978-1-5127-0763-2 (hc)
ISBN: 978-1-5127-0761-8 (e)

Library of Congress Control Number: 2015912819

Print information available on the last page.

WestBow Press rev. date: 08/28/2015

Dedicated to a few good men on my team:

Father - Don

Grandfather - Carl

Sons - Ryan and Jared

Brothers – Steve, Karl, Rob, Duane, Paul, and all CLC brothers

Contents

Introduction

A Legendary Drive

The 1967 National Football League championship is considered by some to be the greatest game ever played. This infamous game became known as "The Ice-bowl," since the game-time thermometer at Lambeau Field read -18 degrees. The wind chill was -50.

Coached by the renowned Vince Lombardi, the Packers began the final drive of the game from their own 32-yard line with 4:50 left on the clock. The scoreboard showed, "Dallas Cowboys 17 - Green Bay Packers 14."

Facing both brutal weather and determined defensemen, the Packers executed a march down the field using a combination of runs and passes. As they approached the goal line the running game was shut down. Time was running out. With only 16 seconds remaining, Green Bay called their last timeout. After consulting Coach Lombardi, quarterback Bart Starr returned to the huddle and relayed the plan from their coach. They were not going to settle for a field goal attempt to tie the game. Starr called a play and approached the line of scrimmage. He took the snap, paused, and then lunged forward behind his center and guard, falling into the end zone and into victory. The Packer fans jubilantly stormed the field, while the frostbitten and utterly exhausted Packer players wept. They finished successfully in the face of great adversity.

The Grind and the Joy

A football scoring drive quite possibly has more parallels to life and faith than any other earthly activity, game, experience, profession or endeavor.

For all of us, life on the field of play blends successfully executed plays with mistakes and hard hits that knock us to the turf. We have injuries, tough breaks and calls that go against us. We have times of progress and times of being tackled for a loss… times of success and times of failure… times of celebration and times of great disappointment.

All men will go through this life with a series of battles between the kickoff and the clock reaching zero. We will be kicked around, knocked down, and bloodied up a bit in the fight with the enemy. Life is difficult, both for the Christian and non-Christian. It's not one huge victory after another. We will have major triumphs along the way. But more often it's an inching forward as we win one small battle and then prepare for the next one. Inch by inch, play by play, we doggedly move ahead – a small success followed by a setback, and then another small victory.

We all need first downs where the past is left behind and a fresh start begins anew. We all need times to huddle with teammates and be encouraged and challenged before facing the opposition again.

In spite of the hits and struggles, many football players play the sport with great passion and joy. A good running back knows he's going to get hit hard, and yet he wants to play. He still wants to carry the ball. He just loves playing the game. Similarly, when we are playing the game of life as it was intended to be played, the hard hits still come at us - but they don't steal our life's passions and joy.

How about you? Are you advancing the ball during your drive down the field of life? Are you continuing to play with passion and love for the game? Is your game plan solid enough to lead you to real victory?

Like the 1967 Packers, you can be joyous and victorious in the face of intense adversity if you play under a brilliant coach, huddle with the best quarterback, rely on your teammates, and follow great blocking.

Keys for Victory

In the scoring drive of life, you're the ball carrier running against eleven determined Spoilers defensemen out to stop you. Each opponent has a different way of bringing you down.

Many teams do not stand a chance of winning against the Spoilers. Yet one team has the right weapons necessary for a victorious outcome. That team is the Followers. The Followers know how to get their running backs down the field and into the end zone. Four reasons for the Followers success include:

1. They know what they are aiming for – they know what victory looks like;
2. They have the needed team leadership and game plan;
3. They keenly understand the tactics of the enemy; and
4. They have the right teammates for knocking down the opposition and opening holes for running backs.

All running backs who accept the call to play for the Followers have the potential to see victory.

Knowing Where to Run

The Packers had one goal as they began their scoring drive -- to reach the end zone. They saw exactly where they needed to go. They knew if they could string together several successful plays and first downs, they would be victorious.

In a football scoring drive, and in life, we need to know what we are striving for. We need to know what victory looks like – both the small victories along the course of the drive and the ultimate victory of reaching the end zone.

Leadership and Game Plan

A successful football team not only knows where they are heading, they have a game plan of how to get there. The Packers were coached by the great Vince Lombardi. He understood what it took to win football games. His approach and game plan usually resulted in success. The Super Bowl trophy is called the "Lombardi Trophy" for good reason.

Victory in life also comes from following brilliance and a solid game plan. Unfortunately, the game plan for many men is ill-defined, misunderstood or inadequate for achieving success. We all need a reliable team leader whose game plan, strategy, playbook, and direction leads to victory. Every man who plays under the Followers has all of this.

Knowing the Opposition

The Packers had to get past eleven elite Cowboys defensemen to reach victory. We all have barriers in the way of our progress down the field of life. We face eleven major forces of destruction and deceit. Eleven starting defensemen for the opposition prowl around the field and wait for the next ball carrier to devour. Most men miscalculate or underestimate the opposition.

Men need to see and understand how life's battlefield is set up. We not only need to see who is on our side to help us down the field, but to also see our adversaries and how they are positioned to stop us. By looking at life through the football metaphor, we put skin on the invisible battles we all face, making it easier to confront and defeat what is stopping us from victory.

Teammates

Nobody succeeds alone. We all need teammates to help us make progress and cross the goal line. The 1967 Packers played as a team. And at the end of the drive, Bart Starr followed right behind his lead blockers to cross the goal line.

In the scoring drive of life, our teammates are absolutely essential. We simply cannot win on our own. Those who carry the ball for the Followers rely especially on the team's Quarterback and Lead Blocker. These two convert the game plan into successful action on the field. Along with the rest of your teammates they want to see you succeed in your drive down the field of life.

Inviting You and Some Teammates

You're invited to be a ball-carrier on the scoring drive of your life. If you play for the Followers, you'll see the path to a life of significance, adventure, freedom, joy, peace, hope and love. You will know what you're aiming for. You'll know the game plan that can successfully get you past the barriers preventing victory. You will be playing with the Ones who can get you there.

Bring some other men with you on this drive down the field to victory. Seek a few men whom you can invite to read this book with you. Read a chapter each week, huddling weekly to explore answers to the chapter's discussion and Bible study questions found online (free) at: www.UltimateScoringDrive.com. The sixteen chapters can be completed over the course of a football season.

Part I
Starting the Drive

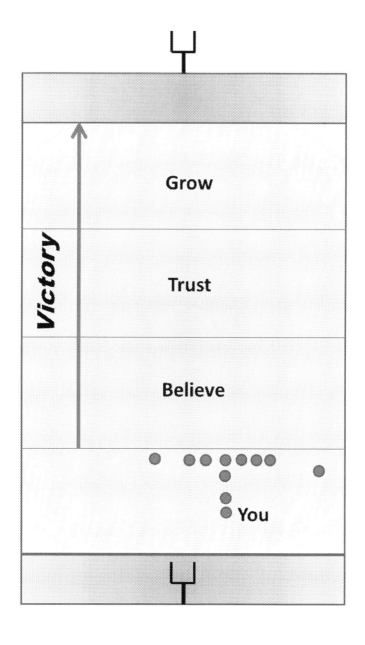

Chapter 1

Playing for the Followers

Where You Started

You were born into a family, a country, a situation that has impacted where you are right now on your drive down this field of life. Some men were raised with largely absentee parents, poor role models, and a history of tragedy and disappointment. Some only heard the words "God" or "Jesus Christ" when someone reacted in anger.

Michael Oher, the Ravens offensive lineman whose story was depicted in the movie *The Blind Side*, had an extremely tough upbringing. In his book *I Beat the Odds*, Oher paints a bleak picture of his childhood. "You're not poor if you know where your next meal is coming from," wrote Oher. "That's one of the first lessons I learned growing up." Raised in a rough part of Memphis, Oher noted, "I never really knew my real father." He describes his mom as an alcoholic and drug addict who often abandoned her kids for long periods. Homeless at times, Michael once lived under a bridge for a couple of weeks. "That was pretty awful," reflected Oher. "No one in my family ever used the words 'I love you.'" Eventually Michael was taken from his mom and family and placed in foster care. "I was a heartbroken little kid who was hurt and confused. . . . I wanted to cry all the time."[1]

Your upbringing likely was better than Michael's. Maybe you were raised by parents who made every effort to provide a loving and stable environment. Seahawks quarterback Matt Hasselbeck said, "I don't have one of those strong conversion experiences where I was a crack addict or something. I was fortunate. I was raised in a home where values were taught."[2] He remembers his parents getting serious about their faith when he was in second grade. "We went to church and Sunday school every Sunday from there on out," said Hasselbeck in an interview for *Sports Spectrum Magazine.*[3]

No matter where you started or where you are right now, we all have a chance to succeed or to fail, to be victorious or to be stopped short of the goal. Quarterback Drew Brees writes, "It is not where you start in life, but rather how you finish."[4] Even if you started out poorly and have not played so well until now, you can still finish victoriously. God makes a victorious life possible for everyone, regardless of starting field position or mistakes along the way.

Michael Oher concluded his book *I Beat the Odds*, with hopeful words:

> "It all comes down to your choices. . . . It's true that we can't help the circumstances we're born into and some of us start out in a much tougher place than other people. But just because we started there doesn't mean we have to end there. . . . You are a unique person created for a specific purpose. Your gifts matter. Your story matters. Your dreams matter. You matter. The decisions you make all matter."[5]

Your choices do matter. And one choice that matters is whether you should slow down enough to carefully consider what this game of life is all about.

Into the Stadium

You may or may not have been raised with a strong Christian influence. You may or may not be a church-goer. You may or may not be a Christian. And if you are a Christian, you may have a stagnant faith or a vibrant faith. Yet, because you have chosen to slow down enough to open this book, you're different than most men. You have come into the stadium and are taking time to examine your life.

Most men lead unexamined lives. The majority of men don't take the time and effort to really determine what is at the heart of this drive down the field called life. We focus on our short-term circumstances, not knowing where we need to run to reach true victory. We are inclined to play the game on our own, hoping our own sheer will is enough to get us somewhere good. Men are generally not keenly aware of who and what is out to stop them from victory, and who would like to help them.

Because you have chosen to come into this stadium where the Followers play, it is likely God has been working on you. It's quite possible that you are in one of three camps:

1) You may be way up in the bleachers with little faith. You sense God trying to get your attention, either gently nudging you or shouting at you through some major life event to come down with Him and His team.

2) You may be down on the sidelines with God's team holding some faith, and God is calling you to a stronger faith and more action on the field.

3) You may already be playing for the Followers with a vibrant faith. You want to make sure that you and those you love finish the game passionately and victoriously.

Regardless of why you have paused long enough to crack open this book, you have come to the right place. Good things happen in this stadium.

Called to Play

Whatever your life looks like at this moment, the God of the universe wants you on His team. As the One in charge of the Followers, He may have drafted you in the past or He may be working to draft you right now. If you are not playing for Him already, He hopes you will answer His call and move from the stadium seats to His team down on the field.

What God really wants is for you to be down on the field running the ball on His team. Anyone can run the ball for the Followers. He will take walk-ons and those rejected from other teams. He'll even take back those men who quit His team in the past. He'll take anyone and everyone who has a true desire to play for Him. It does not matter how talented you are, who you have hurt or what junk clutters your mind and soul. It certainly doesn't matter how smart and capable you feel right now in matters of faith.

God just wants you playing for Him. But He isn't going to force it. He's going to nudge, invite, encourage, and maybe even shake you up a bit to try and get your attention. In the end, though, He waits for you to respond to Him. He will leave you the choice of whether to turn to Him and come onto His team.

You're not meant to just be a fan. You're not supposed to be way up in the crowd, looking down and cheering for Jesus and some tiny-looking players you admire from afar. You're also not meant to be a sideline player, content to be close to the action, but not in it. You're meant to be down on the field with both feet, fully committed to playing the game. When it comes to faith, you're meant to be in the thick of the action -- seeking, knocking, pursuing. God will respond as you pursue Him. He says, "You will seek me and find me when you seek me with all your heart" (Jeremiah 29:13). Jesus said, "Seek and you will find; knock and the door will be opened to you" (Matthew 7:7b).

You may be reluctant to play for the Followers. After all, it may involve some pain, sweat, blood, and sacrifice. It involves risk. There is the risk that this will lead to some sort of change... in the way you think, act, or relate to God. There is the risk that you will be led to give up something... time, control, money, favorite sins, attitudes or something else. There is also the risk that when you see yourself in the bright light of a Holy God, you won't see yourself as clean as you thought you were.

Hall of fame wide receiver Jerry Rice commented on the benefits of taking certain risks. He wrote, "Taking a risk means you are putting something on the line – your security or comfort zone, your reputation, your life – but it also means you have something wonderful to gain."[6]

Hall of fame running back Emmitt Smith similarly concluded that it can be frightening to make a change, but that leaving behind the familiar and comfortable can lead to what is more fulfilling in the end.[7]

When you take the risk to join the Followers you are taking a step toward something incredibly wonderful, and ultimately more fulfilling.

Leader of the Followers

 Sitting in the stands you have access to the Followers playbook, the Bible. In it you start to read about the Followers Team Leader.

The Followers Team Leader is much more than coach, captain, owner, general manager, and commissioner combined. His greatness is hard to fathom.

God leads the Followers, and His ways are not our ways. The Bible says:

> "'For My thoughts are not your thoughts, neither are your ways my ways,' declares the Lord. 'As the heavens are higher than the earth, so are my ways higher than your ways and my thoughts than your thoughts'" (Isaiah 55:8-9).

God understands everything about you, your team and the opposition. He knows things about you that you don't even know yourself. He knows your strengths, weaknesses, tendencies and your full potential. He knows what you're thinking, where you're hurting, and what you're feeling.

With access to every camera angle and every view of the field, He can see exactly how the play sets up and what the opposition is up to. He has a depth of knowledge unlike any other. He knows everything. Yet God won't tell his players everything or answer every question. In time, He will reveal all you need to know to succeed on His team.

The Leader of the Followers wants His players to trust Him even when they cannot reason out crystal clear explanations for everything. You're not always going to know why He calls certain plays. He wants you to have faith without complete understanding, trust without certainty, and obedience without knowing everything He knows.

Those who have played many years for the Followers know that God has his players' best interests in mind. At the essence of His being is love – including a love for every one of His players, and everyone in the stadium.

God wants people to love Him in return. He knows how victorious their lives can become if they do. But He desires real love, a moral heart-felt choice rather than a coerced or programmed reaction. God does not put heartless robots on the field of life. He plays real people with real hearts. He plays you.

The Followers Team Leader leaves you the choice of whether to accept the invitation to play on His team. He allows you the freedom to love Him or not… to follow the team Playbook or ignore it… to follow His instructions or ignore them… to follow your Quarterback's calls or call it as you see fit… to follow your blockers or run off on your own. He will lead you toward victorious choices, but He still gives you the freedom to choose.

Your Team Leader also gives you the option of stopping by for a visit. His office door is always open. He wants his players to drop in and just hang out, or to talk strategy and ask questions about plays in the Playbook. You are welcome with Him any time. Through these times together, as players repeatedly come to Him with questions, needs, uncertainties and troubles, their relationship with Him is strengthened and they build trust in Him.

Talking with the Veterans

 At this point, your reading of the Playbook has inspired you to find out more about the Followers. You choose to come down from the bleachers and onto the Followers sidelines. Some team veterans welcome you and start to converse with you.

Followers veterans have a common attribute. They not only love their Team Leader, but they have this deep kind of respect and reverence for Him. The veterans want nothing more than to please Him and do their part to help achieve team success. The last thing these players want to do is disappoint Him.

The level of respect that Followers players have for their Team Leader is slightly akin to the deep respect that certain NFL players have for their coach.

Tony Dungy is one coach who was deeply respected by his players. Mike Minter, who played for the Super Bowl winning coach, commented on Dungy's life. "Being a Christian isn't part of his life - it is his life. He exemplifies that in everything he says, does, or thinks."[8] Quarterback Peyton Manning said that when he played for coach Dungy on the Colts, the players didn't want to let their coach down. They liked and respected him so much that they just wanted to please him.[9]

Yet the kind of reverence the Followers veterans express about their Team Leader greatly exceeds what is exhibited in the NFL. They revere their Team Leader so much because at the core of His essence is holiness. They have a good sense of how much He loves them. They also know He is infinite in purity, faithfulness, wisdom, power and splendor. Nothing on earth compares to His Holiness. In great reverence, they desire to worship Him, seek His guidance, and just please Him.

Drew Brees has grown to revere the One in charge. Brees writes in his book *Coming Back Stronger – Unleashing the Hidden Power of Adversity*:

> "Fearing God means you have so much love and respect for him that you don't want to let him down and you would do anything to serve him."[10]

This great love and admiration that Followers veterans have for their Leader is contagious. Time spent with such godly men increases the desire to play on their team.

 When asked if you want to go out and carry the ball for the Followers, you pause. Your mind is full of questions and uncertainties. But definitely sensing that the Followers have the right Team Leader, you give a nod and then run out onto the field to join the huddle.

* * *

Huddle questions for Chapter 1 small group discussion are found free online at www.UltimateScoringDrive.com

Chapter 2

Aiming for victory

As you huddle with the Followers offensive squad, you begin to wonder about some things. "How do I win in this game? What should I as a man be aiming for? Which direction do I run for victory?" During a long commercial timeout, you have time to listen to your teammates provide some insight. They share their own life experiences and what they have learned through the team's Playbook.

Knowing the End-game

Football players do not play the game to lose. They clearly know what they are aiming for as they begin an offensive drive. The offense aims for a victory that comes from moving the ball toward the end zone. They know where victory lies and what it looks like.

No man wants to lose in life. But if we don't have a vision of where to run, we will likely end up going backwards, sideways, out of bounds or tackled short of the goal. It helps tremendously if we know where real victory can be found before running too far down the field of life.

Without giving it much thought, many men jump to the conclusion that our aim ought to be centered on achievement, accumulation and accomplishment. But the testimonies of many NFL players indicate that such pursuits are not the answers for living victoriously.

Success in the NFL

Several years ago, Tom Brady, Super Bowl champion quarterback with the New England Patriots, was interviewed on national TV (CBS *60 Minutes, by journalist Steven Kroft*). By that point Brady had tremendous success in the NFL. He was making millions of dollars per year while dating actresses and supermodels. By earthly standards, he had it all. Yet during his interview, Brady surprised many people by admitting that his incredible worldly success was not bringing him full satisfaction. Brady suggested that even after three Super Bowl rings, there had to be much more to life.[11]

Not everyone has had the chance to win Super Bowls and become millionaires; but many men have come to the conclusion that all their earthly pursuits of accumulation and accomplishment are not bringing them true joy, peace and fulfillment. When taking the time to reflect on their life, they discover something major is missing.

Deion Sanders described the desperate emptiness he felt during the pinnacle of his sports career while playing both professional football and major league baseball. Sanders described the situation in his book *Money, Power and Sex – How it almost ruined my life*, writing:

> "Everything I touched turned to gold, but inside, I was broken and totally defeated. . . . I was on my way to being named Defensive Player of the Year. . . . I remember sitting at the back of the practice field one afternoon, away from everybody, and tears were running down my face. I was saying to myself, 'This is so meaningless. I'm so unhappy. We're winning every week and I'm playing great, but I'm not happy.' . . . I had everything the world had to offer, but no peace, no joy, just emptiness inside."[12]

Rich Gannon, NFL's MVP quarterback for the Raiders, had reached his dream of playing in the NFL. "When I finally got there, it wasn't anything like I expected," recalled Gannon in *Sports Spectrum Magazine*. "I had fame, I had the money, I had a new home and a car, and all the things I never had growing up. But I realized there was an emptiness in my heart."[13]

Time and time again NFL players have testified that their fame, worldly possessions and success on the football field are not bringing anything close to real victory in life.

Cultural Success

It's no surprise so many men focus on economic success, material accumulations, and personal achievements. That's generally how our culture judges a man's success inside and outside the NFL.

The worldly culture is likely to declare a man's life victorious if he has an important job with lots of promotions, a good salary, notoriety, a big house, a truck and/or sports car, trophies on the bookshelf, entertaining weekends, and a long list of places visited. Before declaring this kind of life victorious, a few in our culture may also want to see a little more. Some would want to also know that he spends time with family, uses no illegal drugs, stays out of trouble with the law, and is generally honest and friendly. When it comes to faith, our culture's victory mantra is: "Be good enough so that you can feel good about yourself and receive good stuff from God."

How does this view of a culturally victorious man fit with your definition of success? Is such a life truly victorious? Or is it a false sense of victory invented by our culture?

Achieving the cultural view of success starts to touch on some good stuff. There may be some love and some sense of significance and adventure. But deep down the culturally successful man is usually less than fulfilled; less than free; and is often stressed in relationships and the busyness of life. Striving solely for this kind of success will not meet your core needs as a man, nor is it in line with your Creator's hope for your life.

What Men Need

Men are hard-wired with a desire to meet certain core needs. We won't live up to our full potential if these needs are not met.

Significance

One of the fundamental needs of every man is significance. We want purpose and meaning. We want relevance. We want to make a lasting difference; to leave a legacy. We want fulfillment, not emptiness.

Challenge

Men desire challenge. We are wired for achievement and adventure. We thrive when we have problems to solve, battles to fight, and mountains to conquer.

Freedom

Men soar when living with the freedom to be completely authentic and genuine - free from the need of creating impressions about our self. We desire freedom from fears, anxieties, past mistakes, failures, shame, and from being controlled by our own impulses, habits and addictions. We thrive when having the freedom to pursue the passions in our soul.

Love

Men need to feel loved… and to feel valued and validated. We need others to love and share life with. We need companionship, friendship and camaraderie.

Hope

Men need hope for the future. We need to know that the tough times won't last forever; that a better tomorrow is possible. We need to know that this life isn't the end and that there is a greater life on the other side.

Renewal

Men need rest for our souls. We need to cleanse the heart and mind and have the weights on our shoulders lifted for periods of time so we are ready to face the next challenges. We need regular times to temporarily step away and renew.

A victorious life will result in a life that meets all of these core needs. True victory brings significance, challenge, freedom, love, hope and renewal. But does meeting these needs define victory? If I am gritting my teeth in determination to meet my own needs, is that going to lead to victory? Is meeting my needs the goal, or is that just the outcome of a victory centered on something else?

Finding Something Better

The eventual realization that worldly pursuits do not bring victory will prompt many men to search... to search for that something else which will bring them a sense of meaning and peace. Some NFL players who found emptiness and disappointment with the popularity, money and success in football, eventually discovered something that satisfied.

After Deion Sanders hit rock bottom, literally and figuratively as he survived driving his car off a cliff, some godly men shared their faith with Deion. Soon thereafter the all-star athlete wrote that he "found Christ" and received a peace he had not known before.[14]

When Rich Gannon heard the testimony of an American soldier who had lost his arm, leg and eye, Gannon "wanted something he had." "I knew what he had was that inner joy and peace that a relationship with Jesus brings."[15] Gannon found that joy and peace upon turning to follow Jesus.

Sanders and Gannon are but a couple of the many NFL players who have reported a transformed life through following Jesus. NFL linebacker London Fletcher changed from an unapproachable man full of anger and rage, to a man who received the Redskin's top humanitarian honors on multiple occasions. "Once I decided to give my life to Christ," said Fletcher, "it was what I was searching for – that peace, that rest, that joy. I finally found it, and I couldn't get enough of it."[16]

Raider's lineman Steve Wiesnewski came to realize that six straight Pro Bowl appearances, fame, fortune, and other worldly things couldn't fill the void in his life and give him peace. "This led me to seek out those who I knew had that peace, comfort, and contentment," noted Weisnewski in a *Sports Spectrum Magazine* article. After a teammate taught him about Jesus Christ and shared the Bible with him, he remarked:

> "I truly began to understand what being a follower of Jesus Christ was all about. . . . In the Oakland Raiders' facility, I turned over all areas of my life - my past, my present, my future, my fame, my fortune, and my family-to Jesus Christ. I put it all into the Lord's hands and asked for His forgiveness. I surrendered my life to Jesus."[17]

Wiesnewski, along with other NFL players, found that their inner-most needs were met when they turned their heart in the direction of Jesus and followed Him.

Now some of you might be thinking at this point:

> "Good for those guys. They found a way to see some victory in their lives. But that is their way, not my way. Jesus is one option; and it's not my option. What works for me is fierce determination and a self-reliant belief in my own abilities."

The Reverend Billy Graham concludes otherwise. Graham, whose life and ministry has positively impacted millions of lives, does not say that following Jesus is *one* option to help a guy reach *some* victory. He does not say that our needs can be met through *our own* self-reliance. He goes so far as to say, "Christ and Christ alone is able to meet every need of the human race."[18]

Biblical View of Victory

One of the challenges in living this game of life is that no scoreboard displays our score. How will we know when we have arrived… when we are truly successful?

While we don't have numeric scores showing our degree of success, we know what victory is all about because God tells us. The thrust of His message is that victory centers on His Son, Jesus.

The Bible says:

> "But thanks be to God! He gives us the victory through our Lord Jesus Christ" (1 Corinthians 15:57).

This victory through Jesus is not just a little victory, but according to the Bible it is an "overwhelming" victory:

> "Overwhelming victory is ours through Christ, who loved us" (Romans 8:37b NLT).

Jesus does not just take care of one or two challenges we face. He came to give His followers overwhelming victory. Victory through Him allows one to live life in all its fullness. Jesus said, "I have come that they may have life, and have it to the full" (John 10:10b). That doesn't mean He came to remove all hardship and pain. Instead, He came to bring a real and lasting victory despite life's difficulties.

This overwhelming victory through Jesus not only leads to full and abundant living on earth, but also has a crucial eternal element. The Bible says that the goal of our faith is the salvation of our souls (see 1 Peter 1:9). The goal, the end result of a victorious life, includes living beyond this earthly life. It involves being saved for the afterlife in heaven. The Bible says:

> "God has given us eternal life, and this life is in his Son. Whoever has the Son has life; whoever does not have the Son of God does not have life" (1 John 5:11-12).

Through victory in Christ our soul is saved for life in heaven… a tremendous personal eternal benefit. But should victory be all about me, and ensuring my trip to heaven?

While Jesus repeatedly stresses the importance of our own eternal life in heaven, He also emphasizes the need to look outward beyond our own benefits and desires. Jesus tells us to focus life on loving God and loving others. He sums up the Bible's commandments in saying:

> "'Love the Lord your God with all your heart and with all your soul and with all your mind.' This is the first and greatest commandment. And the second is like it: 'Love your neighbor as yourself.' All the Law and the Prophets hang on these two commandments" (Matthew 22:37-40).

Tony Dungy nicely summarizes what the Bible says about a victorious life. Dungy, who won Super Bowls as a Steelers player and later as the Colts coach, wrote in his book *Quiet Strength*:

> "God's Word presents a different definition of success than the world – one centered on a relationship with Jesus Christ and a love for God that allows us to love and serve others."[19]

When we start by loving God and having a relationship with Jesus, we will love and serve others in ways that are more impactful and lasting, with the credit going back to God instead of to our own pride. The Bible emphasizes that both loving God and loving others is vital, but that loving God is our greatest calling, and out of that love we can best love others and help meet their needs.

Your teammates gathered with you in the huddle see that you have an uneasy and slightly confused look on your face. Recognizing that many men have a hard time grasping the essence of a loving relationship with God, they encourage you to hang in there. "The further we march together down the field, the more clear and concrete this will all become," they reassure.

Loving, Transforming, Impacting

The Biblical view of a victorious life is built on a foundation of knowing, loving and following God's Son, Jesus Christ. By following Jesus, God's Holy Spirit renews you and transforms you in the direction of Jesus' likeness. Out of this new heart you are able to most effectively love others and impact their lives.

Victorious living is following Jesus. Victorious living is:

1) Receiving God's love for you and growing close to Him;
2) Allowing God's Holy Spirit to transform your heart; and
3) Reaching out in love and compassion to others.

Victory comes when you first receive God's love for you. Responding to His pursuit of you, you passionately engage in an ever-growing closeness with Him in Christ (see John 6:44 and James 4:8a). It is through knowing God in reverence and in friendship that a trust and obedience grows. You love and enjoy God during your life and know that this love will not be severed by death. Your soul will transcend your time on earth and end up in a place where you can enjoy God forever.

Another aspect of victory involves a change deep within your being... a "transformed heart." Your heart is your inner being - what directs your life. It's the essence of where your actions and attitudes and character flow out from. Through a relationship with God/Jesus, your heart is transformed by God's love and Holy Spirit. Freedom replaces slavery to sin and impulse; hope remains no matter what happens; peace replaces much of our anxiety; humility replaces much of our pride; compassion and self-giving replace much of our self-centeredness; deep-seated lasting joy replaces temporary feel-good moments; and forgiveness replaces bitterness. This transformation not only brings you qualities that you desire for yourself, but gives you a new heart and greater capacity to love and serve others.

Victory is not about trying harder to be good. It is about growing close to God, and out of that closeness you are transformed. A deepening relationship with God gives the Holy Spirit access to our inner being. He can create a new heart in us. It's not that you will be anywhere close to perfect. And God certainly does not want you to feel morally superior to others. You will still be subject to temptations, pride, anxiety and moral failings. But you'll be forgiven by God and living in the freedom of a life connected to eternity and led by the Holy Spirit.

Next, your relationship with God and your transformed heart moves you to love and serve others. People will feel genuinely loved by you. They won't feel judged or inferior by your demeanor. Those you love will feel valued, respected and encouraged. Many will sense the peace you have and see God at work in your life. They will see how victory in your life spills over to drench others with self-giving kindness. Some will want to know the source of what is good in your life and to find the joy you have. They will want to get to know Jesus. As they subsequently pursue their own relationship with Jesus, their heart will be changed. In turn, these new and strengthened believers will positively impact yet more lives. Through it all, God is exalted and glorified. And in the end, you and all followers of Jesus will be together in heaven for all of eternity.

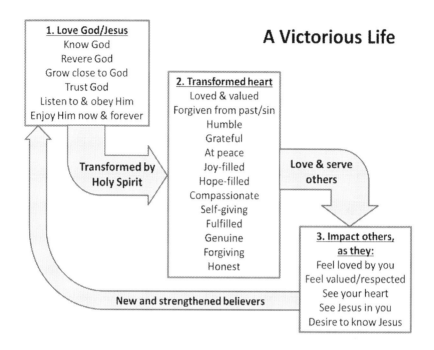

Triumphs along the Way

A successful football scoring drive typically consists of a series of little victories… successful plays, yardage gains, and first downs. A sense of triumph is felt after crossing mid-field, upon reaching field goal range, upon entering the red-zone, and especially after crossing the goal line. Victory in life also involves multiple triumphs… a series of moment-by-moment, day-by-day, week-by-week, and year-by-year victories from following Jesus and surrendering to the Holy Spirit at work within you.

A transformed heart and conquest over the control of sin and death can and often does happen in an instant through the power of God. A huge victory results when you believe in Jesus' love for you and humble yourself before him to receive His Spirit, His love, His grace and His forgiveness. Yet this major time of victory is not a one-time big event that then enables you to coast unchallenged through life. You will have lots of room to grow in knowledge of God and relationship with Jesus. The opposition will continue to tackle you. You will still face many adversaries who do not want you to become more like Jesus and to serve others in His name.

Life is not a single-play, long-bomb into the end zone. The varied experiences encountered during the long drive down the field, as difficult as they can be, are meant to help you grow in your knowledge and love and trust of God. Such life experiences can lead you into a real victory, rather than our culture's shallow and false sense of victory.

Victory in Paralysis

God makes a victorious life possible for everyone, regardless of your upbringing, circumstances, past mistakes, gender, economic status, ethnicity, or health situation.

But what if we can't even walk or talk? Can life still be victorious?

Former NFL linebacker O.J. Brigance shows us that it can. Brigance lived victoriously after ALS (Lou Gehrig's Disease) caused him to lose all control of body movement and speech.

After a long NFL career, Brigance became the "Director of Player Development" for the Ravens. In spite of his extremely healthy lifestyle, at age 37 he was diagnosed with ALS and gradually slipped into paralysis. Only able to communicate through a technology that translates eye movement into words, he remained on staff for the Ravens.

Brigance wrote of his experiences in the book *Strength of a Champion: Finding Faith and Fortitude Through Adversity.*[20] During the tremendous trials of battling his debilitating condition, Brigance grew in his faith. He expressed to the Raven's players, "God uses what the enemy meant to break us, to mold us and strengthen us to be more like Christ." With an ever stronger faith and heart transforming more into the likeness of Jesus, Brigance was determined to help others. He wrote:

"Every triumph and tragedy in my life has served as preparation to stand firm in this moment. To take what many perceive as an unbearable circumstance and be able to impact the lives of others. That's what living is all about."

From his wheelchair and breathing machine, Brigance continued to positively impact lives. Ray Lewis, the Raven's star defensemen, told Brigance that seeing his daily battles with ALS helped him keep life in perspective – never wanting to complain about his own circumstances.

Coach John Harbaugh gained a similar kind of perspective by being around Brigance. Harbaugh's stress prior to Super Bowl XLVII was erased when Brigance was well enough to return from the hospital and come to the Ravens team before the big game. When Harbaugh heard the rattle and hum of Brigance's respiratory machine enter the room, he said "Every concern, every worry – whether it be about the game or life in general – was erased."[21]

O.J. Brigance knows that the challenges he's facing are only temporary. He will land in the end zone of heaven, free from all the pain of this world. He wrote in *Strength of a Champion*, "I learned that as long as Jesus is my Lord and Savior, death had no power over me." Brigance has lived victoriously, not letting his health situation and inevitable end to earthly life stop him. He's victorious through his faith in a Sovereign and Eternal God.

Brigance's story reminds us that victory doesn't mean life will be easy. By following Jesus, we are not promised a life free from heartache and pain, free from frustrations and sadness, or free from persecutions and adversity. But no matter what circumstances and difficulties surround life, deep down a pervasive joy remains. You have an innate sense of peace and fulfillment. You love the camaraderie with your teammates. You know where you're headed.

Pointed in the Right Direction

Your teammates know that success is not wrapped up in personal achievements, financial success, or status. It is not about how comfortable you can make your life; nor is it about how many places you can go. Success as defined by our culture is apt to leave you empty, without the peace, meaning and joy that you long for deep within your soul.

The testimonies of your teammates and the words of the Bible show you what true victory looks like. Victory is found in such a closeness with God through Jesus that your heart conforms toward the heart of Jesus, and your life consequently blesses others in love, honor, respect and service to them. The focus is not on you. The aim is not your personal desires. And yet, the deep yearnings of your soul will be met as a natural outcome. The Bible says, "Take delight in the Lord, and he will give you the desires of your heart" (Psalm 37:4).

A victorious life in Christ brings freedom, significance, challenge, adventure, love, peace and hope. A truly victorious life also transcends this temporary life, extending into an eternal life where we can enjoy God's presence forever.

With a clearer vision of where you're headed, you are now anxious to take the ball and start marching down the field. On 1st and 10 from your own 23-yard line, you receive the handoff from your Quarterback. Immediately you hit a wall of defensive linemen and are tackled for no gain. Shaken by the tackle you stumble back toward the huddle wondering who hit you.

* * *

Huddle questions for Chapter 2 small group discussion are found free online at www.UltimateScoringDrive.com

Chapter 3

A Formidable Opposition

 Shocked by the hard hit during the previous play, you return to the huddle and ask your teammates, "Who are these guys we're playing against?" Your eyes pop open wide as you start to hear about those facing you on the opposite side of the line of scrimmage.

Barriers to Victory

One thing is sure... no matter where you start your drive, opposing forces will be there to try and stop you from a victorious life. Since victory centers on knowing, loving and trusting God, they aim to drive wedges that separate you from God. Separation from God consequently prevents your heart from transforming and reduces the positive impact you can have on others.

Barriers to victory can bring you down at any point on the field. These adversaries come from our culture, from your past, from demonic influences, and simply out of your own fallen state of humanness, brokenness and inherent sin.

We each face eleven starting players of destruction and deceit who play for the Spoilers. The gridiron is strewn with bodies of those injured, paralyzed or nearly dead from these hard hitting players. The Spoilers are coached by a wily and cunning deceiver, Satan. Most of us find the thought of Satan so creepy and repulsive that we would prefer to shut him out of our minds. Yet we can't wage war against his influences if we pretend they don't exist.

The Bible says, "Your enemy the devil prowls around like a roaring lion looking for someone to devour" (1 Peter 5:8b). But the Bible also reveals that the demons are not always appearing to us as roaring lions. It says, "Satan himself masquerades as an angel of light" (2 Corinthians 11:14). Not all of the opposing players initially appear as evil adversaries.

Jesus said of Satan, "For there is no truth in him. When he lies, he speaks his native language, for he is a liar and the father of lies" (John 8:44b). Jesus understood the threat posed by "the father of lies" and he prayed that His disciples would be protected "from the evil one" (John 17:15).

Many weapons of spiritual warfare, especially lies, have been interjected into our culture. We tend to under-recognize the destruction caused by these numerous forces fighting against us.

Your relentless adversaries often hit you when you are tired, worn-down, lonely, stressed or depressed. In a vulnerable state, you will be more apt to fall for their deception. Deion Sanders wrote, "I try to be on my guard at all times against the wiles of the devil because he knows me and knows where all my doors and windows are."[22]

The Spoilers want you separated from God. Each opponent tries to get at you in a different way. They know how to sway you by using trash-talk and mind games to mess with you.

Trash-talk is common in the NFL. The Cowboys hall of fame running back, Tony Dorsett, recalled how some of the defensive players on other teams were down-right nasty. They would say anything to distract players from playing the game, including bad things about opponent's wives, parents, and children. Dorsett said it was "pretty rough stuff."[23]

The Spoilers know your story. They know what distracts you. They use lies specifically fitting for your situation, your past, and your vulnerabilities. They aim to gain advantage over you by distracting you, confusing you, and interfering with your vision.

Defining the Battlefield

The Spoilers starting players typically line up in a 4-4 defense, with four down linemen, four linebackers and three defensive backs. Their corny names reflect the tactic they use to impede your drive down the field.

Defensive Line

The Spoilers front four are such major barriers that you won't have a real saving faith without getting past these brutes. They are going to do everything possible to keep you from humbly believing in and following the Lord.

> The defensive end *"U.R. Isolated"* tries to convince you that God is detached from you and impersonal... that you are disconnected from God. *Isolated* says, "While God may have set this earth in motion, he's certainly not anyone you can talk to, relate to, or love. You are essentially on your own; so don't think you can rely on God to be there for you. You're isolated from Him." *Isolated* knows if you have an incorrect, confused and distorted concept of a detached God, that will bring an incorrect, confused, and distorted response to Him.

M.Y. Pride, the left defensive tackle, wants to keep you away from truly believing and following anything better, stronger, or superior to yourself. This defensive tackle is happy when you're blinded to faith as you seek control, self-sufficiency and self-righteous goodness. "You shouldn't have to bow down to anybody, depend on anyone or relinquish control to anyone or anything, including God," says *Pride.*

The other defensive tackle, *Barry N. Grave,* tries to keep your focus solely on your immediate circumstances. "Even if God exists, don't count on anything beyond this life. God doesn't love you enough to care about your eternity. After you die you won't ever be with God, so why even try to get to know him now. There's no need to pay attention to God," claims *Grave.*

Cliff Impure knows that your impure thoughts and actions are a huge cliff separating you from God. *Impure* first leads you into wrongful thoughts and actions. Then he later convinces you that because of your sin, you should hide from God, avoid Him, ignore Him, or rebel against Him. This defensive end says, "If you just stay away from God, you're going to feel so much better." For those who still want God's favor, *Cliff* switches gears and says, "Ok then... just work and work and work at good things and maybe you can earn God's love for you again."

Your chances of victory will be stopped at the line of scrimmage if you are tackled by any of the front four. To make progress, you must penetrate these four. Defeating *Isolated, Pride* and *Grave* sets you up to humbly accept God's Way of defeating *Impure.* Once you're past *Impure,* you will experience the biggest triumph of your life. You will receive God and believe. But the enemy still has several ways of stifling progress down the field of trusting God and growing into a mature victorious believer.

Linebackers

Beyond the linemen await the trust-hindering linebackers. They distract you with fears, anxieties, disillusionment, resentment and self-gratification. They aim to interfere with victory at all levels, hampering your relationship with God, preventing character growth, and reducing your godly impact on others.

> *Ben Suffering* creates doubts about your good and loving God through the inevitable hurts, tragedy and cruelties surrounding life. "How can God love and care about you in a world with so much suffering? Look at this world full of chaos, destruction, and pain, and then tell me your God is in charge."

> *Max Fear* tries to paralyze your trust in God through fears, worries, anxieties and continuous stress. He wants to leave you with no peace of mind, minimal impact, and separation from God. He wants you to play the game with timidity. "You may fail and become irrelevant. You could lose your job, lose the esteem and respect of others, or even lose loved ones. How can you have peace and trust when life is so uncertain."

> *M.T. Self* leads you away from God and into the empty and disillusioned world of a life focused on yourself. He wants you to listen to his victory-preventing lies. "What you need to do is make sure you are happy. Life is about you, and your interests, pleasures, advancement, achievements, power, accumulations, entertainment, and comfort. I have everything you need for a pleasurable and significant life," he lies.

Red Past breeds anger and bitterness in your heart by leveraging past hurts, betrayals, and injustices. "You are entitled to remain angry at your dad. He was never there for you. Never trust him, and never trust God. Neither can be relied on. That friend and that neighbor slighted you in such a way that you're entitled to remain forever resentful. How can you keep coming to a church whose member treated you that way? Just stay away from God and His church." *Red Past* also hopes that you hold a grudge against God personally. "Why continue talking to God when He didn't come through for you in that clutch situation? How can you trust Him?"

The linebackers stop many men. But by following your team's game plan, you will get past them and grow in your trust and love for God.

Defensive Secondary

The Spoilers three defensive backs use more subtle faith-squelching techniques than the linemen and linebackers. They prevent growth and maturity in your relationship with God, your character, and your loving service to others.

Noah U. Perfect lures you into thinking that this life is all about your performance. Then *Noah* tries to make you feel like a hypocrite through your imperfect life of faith, hoping you become worn down and discouraged. "True Christians don't think those shameful thoughts or do those things. How can you fail to take that action? Either Christianity doesn't work or you're not really a Christian. Get out of the game... It's just not for you."

Rusty Passivity's goal is to get you to complacently go through the motions of faith, falling well short of living all-in for God. *Passivity* wants your faith to gradually rust out. "Attend some church; give a little of your time and money to help others now and then; fit in with the world; avoid doing things that might cause people to reject you; pray sometimes; show love to your family and friends but not so much to others. Then feel very good about yourself. You're better than most. Time to coast."

The other defensive secondary player is the often overlooked safety, *B.N. Busy*. He's seemingly not a threat. But the game films show otherwise. He tackles you throughout your drive. *B.N. Busy* tries to keep you so busy doing things, often good things, that you lose sight of the need to just be with God. "Do good things; keep a full resume; don't slow down; don't say 'no' to demands for your time." *Busy* wants you to stick with a no-huddle offense, not taking time to just be with God and share lives with Him. If you choose that route, your victorious faith deeply rooted in a love for God will start to erode.

Every man is hit by most, if not all, of these eleven opposing players. Some men are attacked by additional players who come off the bench and onto the field to feed on tendencies of addiction, depression and psychological disorders. Such specialty demons are not starting players against every man, but they wreak havoc for certain men. Defeating specialty player demons often requires professional help in addition to a strong faith-life.

Penetrating the Enemy
On his own, no man can get past the eleven adversarial barriers. All men will fall short – tackled continuously by many of the Spoilers players. Fortunately, the Followers Team Leader knows how victory can be accomplished. He has the winning game plan.

The Bible says, "With God we will gain the victory, and he will trample down our enemies" (Psalm 60:12).

To defeat the enemy, you will need the divine power provided when you play for the Followers. The Bible says, "The weapons we fight with are not weapons of the world. On the contrary, they have divine power to demolish strongholds" (2 Corinthians 10:4). The Followers have a game plan that uses this divine power to move the ball down the field through each adversary. The game plan leads you toward the life God wants for you on this earth and an eternal life that's glorious beyond all description.

* * *

Huddle questions for Chapter 3 small group discussion are found free online at www.UltimateScoringDrive.com

Chapter 4

The Game Plan

Knowing more about the Spoilers defensemen, you now recognize the need to understand your team's plan for getting past these brutes. Before you are comfortable receiving the hand-off again, you want to know the plan. So you run off the field to take a closer look at your Playbook and talk further with Coach and teammates.

Carry the Ball

God's game plan is to hand the ball off to you time and time again. You will carry the ball into life's wide-ranging mix of experiences, challenges and difficulties. The varied experiences will help shape you into the man God wants you to be. But you're not going to just be thrown out onto the field alone to get trampled by the enemy. God will lead and help you on the battlefield. He promises all the help you need for success. He gives you the ultimate Playbook. He gives you an extraordinary Lead Blocker, the best Quarterback in the universe, and a host of other great teammates.

Know and Use Your Playbook

The Followers Playbook, the Bible, reveals God's game plan for victory. God doesn't reveal every single thing you *want* to know, but everything you *need* to know. You see the tactics of the opposition. You see how other players before you succeeded and how others lost. Successful plays used throughout the Followers history are described in detail. But more importantly, the Playbook includes descriptions of interaction between the Followers Team

Leader and various players. You see what kinds of relationships with Him led to victory, and how ignoring Him led to utter defeat.

But the Bible is more than a book of strategy. As you read it the pages come alive. God is right there with you, talking to you, challenging you, comforting you, reassuring you, and training you.

Essential Help on the Field

Your Playbook describes how God does not just lead from the sideline or owner's booth above, but His game plan is to be on the field playing with you. In the scoring drive of life, God is out on the field with you - leading, blocking, instructing, and helping. Victory is made possible for you because God comes onto your offense and into your huddle, playing the game with you on every play.

Your Playbook reveals how God always remains your Father in heaven; yet He also comes directly into your life and heart through His Son Jesus Christ and through His Holy Spirit. Our minds cannot fully comprehend this. We have a hard time grasping how God can be three distinct "persons" at the same time, leading from heaven and yet also playing with us out on the field. We look for earthly examples and we can't find anything directly comparable. In football, perhaps the closest similarity is when men serve as both players and coaches at the same time.

Two of the most notable men to serve as player-coaches include Curly Lambeau of the Green Bay Packers and George Halas of the Chicago Bears. Curly Lambeau, who founded the Packers, was the lead runner and passer for the Packers at the same time he coached the team. George Halas played wide receiver and defensive end while coaching the Bears. Halas was also the team's business manager at the same time. Both men held the player-coach role for about a decade and then continued to coach for many more years, each leading their team to six NFL championships.

The player-coach example still obviously falls way-short of conveying the essence of God being in heaven, with us, and in us, all at the same time. When we liken spiritual matters to earthly endeavors such as football, we are always going to inaccurately portray God. God will viewed as too small, too narrow, and too limited. Much about God is mysterious. The full measure of His Holiness and infinite majesty cannot accurately be put into earthly terms.

And when it comes to worshipping God, the Bible says we are not to worship God in earthly terms and objects. "God is spirit, and his worshipers must worship in the Spirit and in truth" (John 4:24).

We worship God in Spirit and only use earthly examples to help us grasp certain elements of our faith-life. We see similarities between our world and the Biblical picture God has painted of His kingdom and the Way to victory. Sometimes these earthly analogies, when constructed in harmony with God's Word, can help us to wrap our mind around the multiple dimensions of our spiritual life.

Again, we don't have an accurate earthly comparison to the trinity of God the Father, Son and Holy Spirit. What we do know from the Bible is that God comes to us on the field of life as His Son Jesus and as His Holy Spirit. His presence with us is essential for moving through the opposition and onto victory. The reasons for this will become more and more apparent as you start to make progress down the field.

Lead Blocker

"On the football field, the unsung player is the fullback," writes Shaun Alexander, the Seahawks All-Pro running back, who averaged 1500 yards per year between 2001 and 2005. "His job is to throw his body in front of oncoming tacklers and protect the running back."[24]

Emmitt Smith, who broke the all-time career rushing record in 2002, gave great credit to his blocking fullback Daryl Johnston. The Cowboys commonly gave the ball to Smith during a play called the "lead draw." The main blocker on that play during Smith's career was almost always Daryl Johnston (also known as Moose). Smith describes in his book *Game On*, how he heard Moose's body collide into the opposing linebackers with such tremendous force that it "sounded like a ten car pileup." Smith often wondered how Moose ever raised himself off the turf.[25]

The key to the Followers success is blocking. To see victory, you need to cling to the jersey of your "Lead Blocker" and follow Him through the holes He creates. God comes onto the field of life as Jesus to serve as if He is your lead blocker on every play. He takes on the belief-stopping linemen, the trust-hindering linebackers, and the growth-halting secondary. Follow your Lead Blocker and you will move the ball downfield past the eleven starting Spoilers and past any additional bench-players that the Spoilers coach sends into the game.

Your victory hinges on whether you closely follow Jesus. Jesus repeatedly told people to follow Him.

> Jesus told Peter and Andrew, "Come, follow me" (Matthew 4:19).

> Jesus told Philip, "follow me" (John 1:43).

> Jesus told Levi, "follow me" (Luke 5:27).

> Jesus told the young rich man to sell everything and "follow me" (Matthew 19:21).

> Jesus said, "Whoever serves me must follow me" (John 12:26a).

Jesus said, "Whoever wants to be my disciple must deny themselves, take up their cross daily and follow me" (Luke 9:23).

Jesus said, "I am the light of the world. Whoever follows me will never walk in darkness, but will have the light of life" (John 8:12).

Jesus said, "My sheep listen to my voice; I know them and they follow me" (John 10:27).

And after Jesus had returned to life, He again tells Peter, "follow me" (John 21:22).

Some people answered the invitation and followed Him – they believed, trusted, and walked with Him. Others did not. The Followers game plan is for you to follow Jesus on every play down the field of life.

The Bible says, "The reason the Son of God appeared was to destroy the devil's work" (1 John 3:8b). When you follow Jesus ever so closely, you see Him accomplish the hard work of destroying sin and all that's in the way of victory.

Most men are tempted to sidestep the enemy on their own without their Lead Blocker. Bad decision. Your fancy moves will only get you so far. If you rely on your moves alone, you will be defeated. You need the One who can absolutely level each of the eleven who are dead set against allowing your progress toward the end zone.

Jesus takes on the weight of the world so we don't have to. You can't carry the opposing players on your back down the field without such enormous weight driving you into the turf. But by following Jesus, He takes the hits for you. He leads the way through the opposition, clearing the path for you to move downfield.

By closely following Jesus and seeing Him in the heat of battles, you may come to realize that your first impressions about Him were wrong. You had heard that He and His friends were too meek and gentle to deal hard blows to the opposition. Playing on His team, you confirm that He is loving, but certainly not docile. He is meek, and yet He's also aggressive. He is at peace, but certainly not passive (see for example Matthew 10:34-36; and Matthew 23:23).

Those who closely follow Him are also loving and compassionate, but are not always as "nice" or as docile as the world would like. Stu Weber in his book *Four Pillars of a Man's Heart*, writes about the commonly held misperception of what it means to follow Jesus. He writes:

> "Christians, if truly Christians, are not always *nice* or *agreeable* in the eyes of everyone. But they are appropriately honest. Truthful, not ugly. Firm, not antagonistic. Persistent, not discourteous. Sometimes being a Christian simply requires that one say the hard thing. Jesus did it regularly."[26] "Jesus is the one who said, 'Do not think I came to bring peace on the earth; I did not come to bring peace but a sword.' Jesus was not about to toss 'peace' around indiscriminately, as though it were some kind of pixie-dust tranquility. He knew better than anyone that ultimate peace would come only as the product of a war on evil. He knew it would come at a great cost. And He was willing to pay it."[27]

Jesus, retains a loving spirit toward others, even when they vehemently disagree with His message of truth and love. But Jesus also realizes that conflict and confrontation is often needed to secure lasting peace. Taking evil head-on, Jesus never considers giving-in or compromising.

Jesus not only leads you down the field through the attacks of the enemy, but He's also on the field to lift you up. After getting tackled, He extends His hand to pull you back up onto your feet. Realizing His deep love for you, and knowing that He has experienced many of your same life struggles, you want to share your heart with Him.

The more time you spend with Jesus the more his contagious character rubs off on you. Over years of playing together, through all the practices and meals, in the locker room, through the tough games and preparation, you not only become close friends with Him, but you're changed by Him. You become a new player, with a whole new passion for the game, for God, for your teammates, and for all people.

The heart of the Followers game plan is to have you closely follow Jesus.

Divine Direction

On the field of life, you need someone who can call the plays, guide you, counsel you, comfort you and give you power, strength and freedom. You need someone who can constantly help you understand what is going on and lead you into all truth. You need someone you can huddle with; and someone who can call audibles when something needs to be changed. When you play for the Followers and truly follow Jesus, you're given such a helper, the Holy Spirit.

No football position directly relates to the work of the Holy Spirit. But one position seems to have more similarities to the Holy Spirit than others – the quarterback. Your quarterback translates the playbook and game plan into action on the field. We are utterly dependent on our quarterback in football, and we are utterly dependent on the Holy Spirit for victory in life.

A good QB knows the background, strengths and weaknesses of His players, and he knows how to lead and inspire them. The Holy Spirit knows you. He's with you always – on the field, in the huddle, in the locker room, on the sideline, everywhere. He never leaves you because He lives in the heart of believers. He calls the plays, provides encouragement, teaches you, confronts and convicts you of your sins, inspires you, and gives you confidence. He sends you in the direction of your Lead Blocker and helps you align your life with Him.

Your "Quarterback's" voice rings in your head as you approach the line of scrimmage… the called play, the snap count, the inspiring words. Then He sees something. He can perfectly read the strategies of the opposition. He adjusts and calls an audible. Listening to Him is critical. Listening in the huddle… listening on the field… listening on the sidelines. You need to tune into His voice… the still small voice of God's Spirit.

You can count on Him. Everything about Him is in union with your Team Leader, Lead Blocker and Playbook. He is the One who works through His players to bring God's eternal plans to fruition. He is God in operation within individual lives. If you hear a play called that's not in the Playbook, you need to ask Him to repeat it, because you heard Him wrong. Your "Quarterback" never calls plays that are inconsistent with the Bible.

When you play with God's Holy Spirit, you experience great joy in playing the game, becoming patient in following your blockers, gaining self-control and self-discipline. He imparts His qualities of love, inner peace, kindness and goodness to you and your teammates.

You feel His power and are able to accomplish things that are just not possible without Him. Your field of vision becomes clear. The whole game starts to make sense. You know where you're heading. You're being led on the field by the Ones who can get you there. Relinquish control to Jesus and the Holy Spirit will come to you. Together they will be with you on the field of life, working in unity with God the Father to lead you on to victory.

Other Teammates

The Followers game plan includes surrounding you with other teammates… imperfect people who are trying through the power of the Holy Spirit to live as Christ lived. They truly desire to help you cross the goal line with the ball tucked safely in your arms. You need these teammates.

Joe Montana, hall of fame quarterback for the 49ers, wrote that in his opinion we are more dependent on our teammates in football than in any other sport.[28] The great running backs also know the importance of the rest of the team. Hall of famer Barry Sanders, after being the 3rd person ever to gain 2000 yards in a season, emphasized that he did not do it alone. He gave thanks to God and to his many teammates who blocked for him. Sanders recognized that without his teammates he would not have run very far.[29]

Your teammates may be your friends, wife, and family who are followers of Christ. They also include pastors, priests, church leaders, coaches and mentors. They are authors, musicians, radio hosts, scientists, psychologists, painters, retirees, volunteers, and a whole bunch of others who help you in your walk of faith.

These other teammates are not Jesus, and you should not expect them to be Jesus. They are not perfect as Jesus is perfect. Nonetheless, you see how God works through their lives and you get fired-up playing with them. You get to know God better in some way because of their lives. Many teammates give you help, support, and encouragement in this challenging world to navigate.

Some of your teammates will have character resembling that of Cowboys hall of fame quarterback, Roger Staubach. Running back Tony Dorsett played many years with Staubach. Dorsett wrote in his book *Running Tough*, that while he sometimes had chosen to live a different lifestyle than Staubach, he maintained such respect for Staubach that he would want his son to grow up to be like him. Dorsett said that Staubach was "a true Christian" who highly respected his teammates, and was always ready to help other teammates in any way he could. Staubach's will to excel and to win "lifted the whole team," according to Dorsett. He was a man of "class." Dorsett concluded that playing with Roger on the Cowboys was "something special."[30]

Wow... what a blessing to have a teammate like Roger! When it comes to faith, the opposing coach would prefer that you remain on a small island disconnected from such teammates. He knows that if he can isolate you from the rest of the team and have you form your faith on your own, you are like clay that can be smashed and reformed.

The Spoilers try to tell you, "Faith is a highly personal matter... it's between you and God. You don't need anyone else's opinions, challenges, or questions about your walk of faith. You are strong. You've got this figured out. You don't need the church. You can do this faith thing all on your own. Organized religion is full of hypocrites and problems. Just keep to yourself."

If the Spoilers can keep you away from your Followers teammates, they know they can win. It will be harder for you to maintain a strong commitment to faith when you're not in the company of other believers. You'll have less encouragement and accountability. You will not be sharing your faith with others or building them up during their walk of faith. You'll succumb more easily to temptations - straying, drifting, slipping. And the enemy can more easily gain leverage from your doubts and fears.

On your own, you're at high risk of fumbling. We need the company of other Christians on our drive down the field. "Let there be no error in our thinking: No man can live the Christian life alone," writes Patrick Morley, author of the best-selling book *The Man in the Mirror.*[31]

Ravens Super Bowl champion linebacker Peter Boulware understands the importance of having godly teammates. He stated:

"The thing that has helped me is to have other Christians, other believers, to keep me accountable. If I were pretty much out there on my own, it would be very difficult."[32]

Derrick Mason, fifteen year wide receiver and kick return specialist for the Titans and Ravens, noted: "It's wonderful, especially being surrounded by a Christian family, Christian people, teammates, and pastors. People to keep you accountable - people that keep you on the straight and narrow." Mason said that it helps to meet with other Christian teammates:

"We try to stay grounded in the Word. We all get together for about an hour or hour-and-a-half, just talking about the Word. . . . It's great to have Christian people around you who truly care about you… making sure you're walking right, making sure you're doing the things God wants you to do."[33]

Some men avoid church and other believers because they think their faith, prayer life and biblical understanding are minimal compared to others at church. They don't realize that nobody needs to wait until they cross some spiritual threshold before getting involved in a local church. The church is a place where you meet people at all field positions. Church is not just for those who have made it into the red zone. It's not a fortress for saints; but rather a home for all, where imperfect and broken lives gather to heal. Have you let the enemy deceive you into thinking you can march down the field without your teammates, and without the church?

Men need other men. You are not meant to go into battle alone. The Bible says, "Let us not neglect our meeting together, as some people do, but encourage one another" (Hebrews 10:25a NLT). You need the rest of your team. They will encourage you, and you will encourage them. We need fellow warriors, men to fight with us at our sides.

Stick with the Game Plan

The Followers game plan is to give you the ball one play after another. Your job is to study your Playbook, listen to your Quarterback, follow your Lead Blocker, and surround yourself with a bunch of Followers teammates. If you stick to this game plan, the opposition will not be able to beat you.

Be careful not to veer away from the game plan. In today's culture of instant everything, we begin to think that we are entitled to immediately hold a deep faith and resolve all our problems. We don't like to take the time to gradually grow in faith as we grind it out play after play. We forget we are not entitled to a quick score.

Too many men decide to follow God's game plan for a while but then later drift away. If you give up following God's plan for victory, you will be tackled hard – potentially so hard that you will cough up the ball to the Spoilers. Victory comes by tenaciously sticking with the game plan, even if it doesn't seem to always be working.

The Bible says, "And let us run with perseverance the race marked out for us" (Hebrews 12:1b). It's an endurance event. We are in it for the long haul. It's not a single play or a short series of plays; it's a long grinding drive that requires grit, determination and perseverance. Each day we battle our human weaknesses, temptations and the lies of Satan's players. We need to keep trusting in God's game plan - reading the Playbook, listening to our Quarterback, following our Lead Blocker, and sticking with our teammates.

Stu Weber concludes in *Four Pillars of a Man's Heart*:

> "God-honoring men stay at it. And stay. And stay. And stay. Growing and improving. Taking the hits and

pushing on down the field. Moving in one direction over the long haul. Many times it's two steps forward and one step back. But it's still movement. It's keeping on keeping on."[34]

Nothing is quick and easy concerning the Christian's march down the field. "When God wants to make a mushroom, he does it overnight, but when he wants to make a giant oak, he takes a hundred years," writes Rick Warren.[35]

As you start running the ball, don't expect to break loose and sprint to the end zone. Brace yourself for a long drive. You're going to get hit and hit again. Follow your Lead Blocker. Go back to the huddle with Him. And then Follow Him again... and again... and again - hour after hour, day after day, week after week. You won't always feel like your faith is working the way it's supposed to. Keep trusting and He will enable you to penetrate each Spoilers player, moving you down the field in the ultimate scoring drive.

Now, with an understanding of the general game plan, you return to the huddle, awaiting your Quarterback's directions. He steps into the huddle and says He's going to send you right toward one opposing player and then another. One by one the tactics of the enemy will be exposed and you will see how your Lead Blocker leads you through each starting Spoilers defenseman. You will first face the defensive front four. The defensive linemen are barriers to believing the Biblical view of an eternal, sovereign, death-conquering, and merciful God Whom you can know and draw close to. Each defensive lineman is a huge obstacle to a victorious life.

* * *

Huddle questions for Chapter 4 small group discussion are found free online at www.UltimateScoringDrive.com

Part II.
Penetrating the Defensive Line-Believing

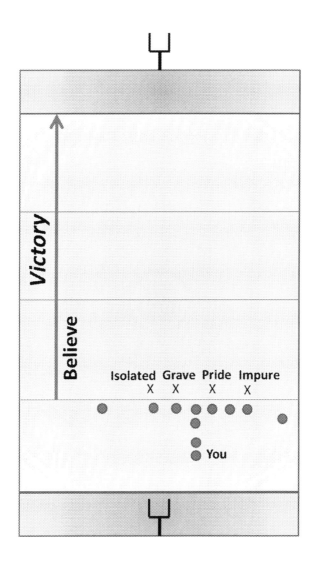

Chapter 5

Annihilating "Isolated"

 2nd and 10 from your own 23-yard line, your Quarterback calls for an off-tackle run. You get the handoff and head right into the hole. The hole closes instantly and you're hit hard by the defensive end, U.R. Isolated, one of the front-four belief stoppers. No gain.

Did Your Maker Leave You?

The Bible says, "Since the creation of the world God's invisible qualities – his eternal power and divine nature – have been clearly seen, being understood from what has been made, so that people are without excuse" (Romans 1:20).

We see this divine power and intentionality in our human emotions and senses. Our soul is stirred by beautiful music. God gives us senses to enjoy pleasurable tastes and smells, humor, and majestic sights. He made us to love others and enjoy companionship with them. God also gives us a sense of right and wrong - moral convictions that lead us to make personal sacrifices to help others.

Did God give us all these pleasurable and loving senses and then not want any part of seeing how we react to these gifts? Did He just leave us to figure out this life on our own without Him?

The Spoilers defensive end, *U.R. Isolated*, says, "You betcha he did." *Isolated* does not argue about whether we had a creator. Instead, *U.R. Isolated* emphasizes the lie that God split the scene after he made earth and people. He knows that most people can clearly see divinity's signature all over nature and human life.

We notice that the world was created with unimaginable order, patterns, colors, beauty and design everywhere -- from the microscopic view of infinite snowflake crystal shapes to the telescopic view of spiraling galaxies. The master artist gave us the plumage of the wood duck and peacock; brilliant sunsets; red maples in the fall; the queen angelfish in the reef; the stripes in a Lake Superior agate; and the giraffe's jigsaw puzzle pattern.

It's easy to be like most Americans and believe in God. But did this God of creation make all this intricate beauty and then vanish from us forever?

"Yep," *says U.R. Isolated.* "God is like a watchmaker. He built the watch, wound it up, and then just set it down to let it tick-on indefinitely without further handling it."

God placed us on the perfect planet. The air has just the right fraction of oxygen to support life but yet not so much that all combustible substances explode. Everything is perfectly harmonized for life, including the earth's tilt, orbit, rotation, proximity to the sun, gravimetric pull, and atmospheric thickness. We have the perfect moon to create ocean tides, circulating the water and replenishing oxygen to support the foundation of our food chain, plankton. We have fresh water distributed throughout much of the globe. We have trees for fire, shelter and replenishing oxygen. We have over 150 minerals, including various metals like copper for routing electricity and iron for plowing the fields for crops. The ground-up minerals make perfect soil for growing food. From seeds, we are able to grow apple trees, corn and enough food to feed billions of people. Gas, oil and coal are situated in underground reserves, waiting to be extracted and used for bringing warmth, energy and transportation to move food and resources around the world.

Did God make the perfect planet for intelligent, relational life to thrive, with no intention of reaching out to us?

U.R. Isolated whispers, "God is not involved in the ongoing affairs of life on earth... especially not you. He's impersonal and detached from the human experience."

Every day miracles abound. Caterpillars morph from legged worms into beautiful winged creatures that can fly between Minnesota and Mexico. Birds not only fly, but have built-in knowledge of where to migrate thousands of miles away. Bees know exactly how to team up and gather the nectar and make the honey. A whale has an automatic system to adjust to immense underwater ocean pressures.

Even our human bodies are living, breathing, walking miracles. Your eyes take in light and convert that light to chemical impulses which travel to the brain to produce a color, 3-D image in a microsecond. Your brain stores much more than 100 trillion facts and handles 15,000 decisions a second. Your body of over one hundred trillion cells started from a one-celled fertilized ovum. As the cells multiplied in your body, they organized themselves into a brain, skin, teeth, lungs, stomach, tongue, liver, etc.. During the miracle of birth, you switched from complete dependence on the umbilical cord to independent breathing and eating. Your body was built to fight off most invading bacteria and viruses, to heal from cuts, and to reroute clogged arteries.

Did the creator of all these miracles decide to go elsewhere in the universe, just as our soul cries out to know our maker?

Getting frustrated, *U.R. Isolated* approaches the line of scrimmage opposite you and says:

> "Listen. There is no god intelligently affecting the affairs on this planet and having a part in your life. You're so alone… God does not care about you one iota… You can't find God or know Him. There is no sense in even seeking him or talking to him, because he's impersonal and he's nowhere to be found."

U.R. Isolated knows that even if he can't stop you completely, perhaps he can hit you so hard that he will damage your helmet, creating a crack of doubt that will make you more vulnerable to the onslaught of his Spoilers teammates.

Personally Connected

God's Playbook for life makes it abundantly clear that *U.R. Isolated*'s words are as empty as a football stadium on a Wednesday evening in March. Your Creator wants to be involved in His creation's life, in your life. The heart of Christianity is a close relationship with God. He wants this closeness with you so you feel loved, blessed, at peace, fulfilled, and never isolated on the field of life.

Because we were made in God's image (Genesis 1:27), God has many of our same personal dimensions. Both man and God: think, feel, love, desire, hurt, and enjoy. God desires a deep personal connection with us and knows how badly we need it. He doesn't just want you to know *about* Him and His moral laws, He wants you to know Him closely and personally. We were made to have fellowship with God the Father and with his Son, Jesus Christ (see 1 John 1:3).

Jesus stresses the importance of knowing God, stating, "Now this is eternal life, that they may know you, the only true God, and Jesus Christ, whom you have sent" (John 17:3a). To have a close relationship with God, we need to get to know God. We can know of God's power, majesty, wisdom and might by seeing His created world. But God's plan was to enable us to know Him personally… to reveal Himself in such a way that we don't just know His power, but we know His heart, such that our heart and His heart connect.

God does not want to be just another acquaintance. He does not want to have a business relationship, where we serve Him and obey Him as best we can in exchange for material blessings. He does not want you just close enough to Him to receive a few benefits, but far enough away that nothing else in your life will change. He does not want a casual friendship, someone you can hang out with when you feel like it, and ignore when you're not in the mood. He also does not want a legalistic, routine and dutiful relationship, where you concentrate on the rules and not on Him.

What God does want, as A.W. Tozer puts it, is "the sweet and mysterious mingling of kindred personalities."[36] We are created for companionship with God… to come into the holy presence of the Living God. God is persistently inviting you into relationship with Him.

God interacts

God started to reveal His heart, His more personal nature, thousands of years ago to the Hebrews/Israelites/Jews. God's character was revealed as He interacted with these people over the centuries. He ensured that written accounts of these interactions were recorded and accurately copied from one generation to the next. Old Testament stories give us a picture of who God is. We see the character of God as: personal, sovereign, holy, eternal, infinite, wise, righteous, just, loving, grace-filled, merciful, faithful, all-knowing, all powerful and ever-present.

God worked with Jews and Israelites to try and set them apart; to try and make sure they did not mix with the false gods of other tribes and peoples. The one true God wanted revelations about Him clearly distinct from made-up notions of gods embraced by surrounding cultures.

Throughout these Old Testament times, before Jesus was born, God emphasized the importance of knowing Him. He stated through the prophet Jeremiah, "Those who wish to boast should boast in this alone: that they truly know me and understand that I am the Lord who demonstrates unfailing love and who brings justice and righteousness to the earth, and that I delight in these things" (Jeremiah 9:24 NLT). The Bible similarly emphasizes the importance of knowing God in Hosea 6:6, where it says, "I want you to show love, not offer sacrifices. I want you to know me more than I want burnt offerings" (NLT).

Some people really got to know God in these pre-Jesus times. King David understood God's desire for relationship. David yearned to know God above all else, with a hunger and thirst for God that brought him to such a closeness that he shared everything with God. David writes, "One thing I ask from the Lord, this only do I seek: that I may dwell in the house of the Lord all the days of my life, to gaze upon the beauty of the Lord and to seek him in his temple" (Psalm 27:4). His writings in the Psalms show us how we can relate to God straight from our heart.

Throughout these Old Testament times God was working toward a plan that would help many more people know Him in much more personal and direct way. God's game plan was to hit *Isolated* real hard, taking him out of the game. God's plan would forever change the way people experience a relationship with Him.

God Comes onto the Field With Us

At God's chosen time in history, He came onto the field and personally entered the game. God came in bodily form to play the game with us, revealing Himself through Jesus' life, words and actions. Since that time, the way people have come to know God most personally is through God's time on earth as Jesus Christ and the presence of God's Holy Spirit in all who follow Jesus.

U.R. Isolated would prefer that you think of Jesus as just a nice, moral guy who was only human. *Isolated* says, "Through Jesus, you can know a great teacher of moral standards, but you plainly can't know God through him or any other man."

Yet Jesus and the Bible emphatically say otherwise. The Bible says Jesus is the "visible image of the invisible God," (Colossians 1:15); the "radiance of God's glory and the exact representation of God's being" (Hebrews 1:3).

Jesus illuminated the nature and glory of God. We could see Him in action, see how He handles the opposition, see how He acts and reacts, see who He befriends, and hear what He says.

The Bible says that God "made his light shine in our hearts to give us the light of the knowledge of God's glory displayed in the face of Christ" (2 Corinthians 4:6b). We see God by looking at Jesus' face shining in our hearts. "All this is a gift from God, who brought us back to Himself through Christ" (2 Corinthians 5:18a NLT). Through Jesus, we are "brought back" into the relationship with God that was separated starting with Adam and Eve.

Isolated hopes you don't open your Playbook and see how often Jesus said He was one with God the Father. The Bible records Jesus' saying:

> "I and the Father are One" (John 10:30);

> "Anyone who has seen me has seen the Father" (John 14:9b);

> "If you really know me, you would know my Father as well" (John 14:7a);

> "… I am in the Father and the Father is in me" (John 14:10a).

Jesus even said, "Before Abraham was born, I am!" (John 8:58). Because Abraham was born roughly 2000 years before Jesus was born, Jesus is emphasizing his own divine nature.

The Bible's New Testament tells stories about the powers of God which Jesus held during his time on earth. Jesus said that all authority under heaven and on earth had been given to him (see Matthew 28:18-20). Jesus commanded the wind to stop, raised people from the dead, forgave sins, and miraculously healed people. The Bible states, "For in Christ all fullness of the Deity lives in bodily form" (Colossians 2:9). He was fully human and fully God at the same time.

Jesus' enemies accused Him of blasphemy, of making himself out to be God. This "blasphemy" was the excuse the Jews cited to crucify Him. The fact that He was put to death at the request of the Jewish leaders is consistent with His claim to be God.

Jesus is God incarnate. God did not detach from His created people. He is not isolated from us. He came to us. We can relate to God in a real and personal way through Jesus Christ.

In one of the most incredible statements in the Bible, Jesus says, "On that day you will realize that I am in the Father, and you are in me, and I am in you" (John 14:20). We are connected with God… in an intimate way. Jesus is in His followers and His followers are in Him.

God Befriends Us

Jesus' friend and follower, John, wrote:

> "And we know that the Son of God has come, and he has given us understanding so that we can know the true God. And now we live in fellowship with the true God because we live in fellowship with his Son, Jesus Christ" (1 John 5:20a NLT).

Through Jesus and the power of the Holy Spirit, we can live in fellowship with God. We can be in friendship with Divinity. Jesus' follower Paul similarly wrote, "So now we can rejoice in our wonderful new relationship with God because our Lord Jesus Christ has made us friends of God" (Romans 5:11 NLT).

One way to begin to understand what God might mean by "fellowship" with Him is to look at close earthly friendships. Some football teammates grow so close to each other that they are more like brothers than friends. They share life at a deep level, being drawn into relationships through the training camps, practices, games, locker room experiences, and rooming, eating and traveling together. There is a connection extending well beyond what teammates say to each other and what they do together. They connect as brothers… as kindred spirits.

One of the most well-known friendships in the history of the NFL was between Gale Sayers and Brian Piccolo of the Chicago Bears, a relationship depicted in the movie "Brian's Song." Piccolo and Sayers became the first black and white friends to room together on the Bears. Their relationship grew closer and deeper as Piccolo helped Sayers recover from a football injury, and as Sayers stayed at Brian's side throughout Piccolo's battle with cancer. They developed a bond so strong that even after Piccolo's death, Sayers said that his friend was "always there."[37]

Differences obviously exist between human relationships and the type of reverent relationship we hold with God. Yet in both there is a loving familial interaction. You spend time together, share lives, and cherish one another. You listen to each other intently and enjoy the company of one another.

Jesus wants us to approach Him heart-to-heart, with total candor and honesty. In addition to our times of reverence and solemnity with the Lord, we can express joyous exuberance, adoration, praise, and even our irritability, resentfulness and frustration. When we are having difficulties we can approach God like a friend and say, "Jesus I'm hurting. I need you. I need your wisdom, your help, your strength."

Like other relationships, this type of life-sharing can be uncomfortable and unnatural in the beginning. But as the friendship develops and grows, so will the desire to spend more time with Jesus. Committing time to Him becomes less about guilt and more about love, responding to God's unending love for us.

He Still Plays the Game with Us

U.R. Isolated doesn't give up. "Even if you insist that God came here as a person 2000 years ago, that was then, this is now. He's not with you today," adds *Isolated*.

Reading your Playbook you see God's words, "Never will I leave you; never will I forsake you" (Hebrews 13:5). God was not about to create His people with a heart and soul and capacity to love, and then reveal himself as Jesus during a short life, only to leave His people thereafter isolated from Him. Jesus said, "I am with you always, to the very end of the age" (Matthew 28:20b).

Two-thousand years after God personally came onto the field of play, we still know God in a direct and personal way through Jesus. Not only do we have the Words of Jesus and His life recorded in the Bible, but God's Holy Spirit is actively engaged in the inner being of all who follow Jesus. Jesus said that God has given us the Holy Spirit, a helper, who will "be with you forever" (John 14:16b). When you follow Jesus, the Holy Spirit will actively work in your life to teach you things and guide you into the truth of God's Word. The Spirit gives you power to know God's will, to live in faith, to resist evil, and to bring healing (see John 14:16; John 16:7; and Acts 1:8).

Jesus said, "I am the light of the world, whoever follows me will never walk in darkness, but will have the light of life" (John 8:12). That light is God Himself on the field with you – as Jesus and as God's Holy Spirit. You are not alone. He is with you.

When you sense you're given wisdom or power in response to prayer, know that it is God with you. When you experience an inner peace beyond explanation, know that the light comes from Jesus and the Holy Spirit. When you "coincidently" run into someone who is there to help you with something you have been praying about, know that God is at work in your life. When you witness lives greatly transformed through faith, know that God is active in the lives of His people.

When you read a passage of the Bible at a time when the words "coincidentally" fit perfectly with your recent struggle, know that God is engaged in your life. Bible study for the Christian is not a mere intellectual exercise, but an encounter with the living God.

When the Holy Spirit makes the scriptures come alive, the Bible becomes a means of experiencing the beauty and glory of God as He shines His light into our hearts (see 2 Corinthians 4:6).

God assures us:

> "...that neither death nor life, neither angels nor demons, neither the present nor the future, nor any powers, neither height nor depth, nor anything else in all creation, will be able to separate us from the love of God that is in Christ Jesus our Lord" (Romans 8:38-39).

Nothing can separate Jesus' followers from the love of God. God is not isolated from you – He's on the field with you, in the huddle with you, playing the game with you, and knocking out the opposition in front of you. You are never alone. God will never leave you. The Creator of the universe wants to share daily life with you. He wants you to know Him and to love Him, and be with Him always.

Everything we need for victory we find in following Jesus. Jesus Christ annihilates *"U.R. Isolated."* Follow your Lead Blocker and *Isolated* will hardly be able to lay a finger on you. Follow Jesus and you will know God – you will know Him personally and have Him with you always.

On the previous play the defense was called for too many men on the field. 2nd down and 5 from your own 28-yard line. The next play is designed to send you back in the direction of Isolated, but this time ensuring that he will not be in on the tackle. Your Quarterback gets the ball and drops back to pass. You cut right and then roll left for a screen pass as your pulling guards set up ahead of you. Isolated reads the screen and stops his rush on the QB, shifting to cover the screen. Your Lead Blocker lines up as a pulling guard and heads straight for Isolated. Isolated is knocked to the ground, enabling you to pick up about three yards before being tackled by M.Y. Pride at the 31-yard line.

* * *

Huddle questions for Chapter 5 small group discussion are found free online at www.UltimateScoringDrive.com

Chapter 6

Leveling "Pride"

3rd and 2 from your 31. You catch a short pass and cut to the outside and make several nifty moves, picking up 7 yards and a first down at the 38. It felt good. "Man, I really made it happen," you think to yourself. The next play is designed to be run off-end, but thinking you know better where the hole is likely to open, you take the ball down the middle. This time the outcome is different. The defensive tackle Pride reads you all the way and hits you for a 2-yard loss. 2nd and 12 from your own 36.

A Mountain to be Moved

M.Y. Pride is a massive mountain of muscle on the defensive line. He gets in on more tackles than anyone. Yet running backs keep heading his direction time and time again, not realizing that by running into him they are not going to get anywhere.

Our pride gets in the way of everything good that God wants for us. Pride moves us to bow down before ourselves rather than before our Creator. It dampens relationships, getting in the way of loving God and loving others. It moves us to judge and exclude others rather than serving and embracing.

Some of you may be pride-fully thinking this chapter does not really pertain to you… after all it's mostly other guys who struggle with pride. Others of you realize that every man struggles with pride, and you know this applies to you. Yet you are uneasy about the possibility of interfering with what you have grown to like -- your opinion of your self, your self-sufficiency, your ego and self-importance.

You may not really want to deal with this misleading enemy, but stay in the game. Don't head to the sidelines or back up into the bleachers. Dealing with the universal problem of pride is so critical that the other opposing players can't be defeated unless you get past *M.Y. Pride*. Victory depends on getting pride under control.

"Wait a minute," *M.Y. Pride* interjects. "Pride is not bad. Shouldn't a man should be proud of many things, including himself?"

In only a few instances does the Bible use the word "pride" to represent something good. The apostle Paul writes to the church in Corinth:

> "I have the highest confidence in you, and I take great pride in you. You have greatly encouraged me and made me happy despite all our troubles" (2 Corinthians 7:4 NLT - see also 2 Corinthians 5:12; 8:24; and Galatians 6:4).

If you see the hand of God in your accomplishments, and see those triumphs as the result of God working in you and through you, there can be a healthy satisfaction or "pride." This can be felt as a pride in your family, someone you mentored, your church, the character of your kids, or an achievement at work, church or home. A healthy "pride" comes when you see God at work in your efforts, and you feel good about how God has used the abilities and life-experiences He gave you to fill a need in this world. Your heart gives God the credit.

The kinds of pride that *M.Y. Pride* promotes are different beasts altogether. Most types of pride create a huge barrier between us and God, between us and victory. It's best to go into the game having done your homework on *M.Y. Pride* to more clearly understand his tactics.

Pride's Many Moves

One of the uglier types of pride is arrogance. Arrogance is so common in the NFL that articles are written about the top 25 most arrogant players and coaches. We see it in the way some players act on the field and their remarks and actions off the field. We see it in how they shirk others and show disrespect. Football fans seem to know arrogance when they see it. But pride also shows itself in less obvious ways. *Pride* nails us with several different moves, each deadly to making progress down the field of life and faith.

Pride of Control

Our pride desires to keep away from anything better or stronger - anything that might make us feel small. We want to think that we are in charge. The thought of someone or something else being in control makes us uneasy. "You shouldn't have to bow down to anybody," says *Pride*. "You should have things run the way you want. Certainly don't relinquish control to God."

Pride spouts off at the line of scrimmage, trying to capitalize on your own natural inclination to be in control. "You are the one really in control… The only one you should obey is yourself… You know what is best." On and on he goes. You start to believe him. No longer do you view *Pride* as the enemy. In fact you kind of like what he's telling you. Puffing your chest you say, "Yeah… I'm the one who knows best. I don't need to look up to anybody or anything."

With those ideas echoing in your mind, you are reluctant to get too close to God. "Why get to know Him? That will only make me feel smaller," your subconscious considers. "I will then need to obey somebody else. I will then need to approach God with something other than a list of questions, demands and concerns. I will need to give up the reigns to someone greater than I. Man… that goes against the grain."

The need to be in control is the direct opposite of faith. When we want to be god of our life, we will not make room for the only God - the God of the Universe, of the Bible, the One who saves us from ourselves. When we try to be God, we veer into Satan's territory, as he desired the same thing.

Pride of Self-sufficiency

As long as you think you're self-sufficient, you cannot know God; for a proud person is always looking down on things and failing to see that which is above.

Pride understands that you, as a man, are quick to convince yourself that you can make life work without anyone else's help. "You don't need to ask anyone for directions," says *Pride*. "You don't need to lean on anybody, including God. You can figure out your own problems... You can do it on your own," he lies. "Besides, your wife and friends will think you are weak if you have to depend on something or someone else."

When you do accomplish something, *Pride* is there to say, "You are the star... you did it... all by yourself." He wants the spotlight on you, not on God.

M.Y. Pride uses your own desire to live independently from God to create a wedge that rebels against God's will for your life. The root of so much of our sin is really self-sufficiency – thinking we can maintain independence from God.

Pride of Goodness (self-righteousness)

M.Y. Pride knows that the hardest nine words to come out of man's mouth are the reconciliatory words, "I was wrong... I am sorry... please forgive me." Our pride makes it hard to admit our mistakes.

The prideful man convinces himself that he's really good, and certainly not in any need of character-strengthening change. His fragile ego would prefer to live in the fantasy of his own goodness. He won't seek friends to challenge or confront him. He won't seek the church and the companionship of believers. The pride-filled man constantly fights to avoid or resist any criticism, any slight, any touchy word that might be spoken against him by friends, enemies, or the God of the universe. He drifts away from God, lost in his tallying marks of good things he has done in his life.

Do see yourself yet in any of these types of pride?

Pride of Self-importance

Pride says, "You're a very important person. Not only that, you're almost always right. You deserve a place of high honor." Continuing on, *Pride* tries to convince you that you should not think of yourself as equal to others, but rather as better, more knowledgeable and more important. "You should freely and smugly give advice because you have the answers and solutions," adds *Pride*. The pride of self-importance leads you away from the One who keeps your self-importance in proper perspective.

When such pride reigns, we don't read our Bible much. And when we open it we are not reading with a spirit of truth-seeking openness, but rather with prideful cynicism. We desire to be smarter than God's Word and to pick and choose what we think must be right and true.

Pride of Religion

Pride does not just show up in the non-church settings. It rears its ugly head in religion as well. "You observe the religious rituals and commandments better than they do," spouts *Pride*. "Just think of all the good works you do... all the money you give... the high quality of your faith-life." *M.Y. Pride*'s poisonous words continue: "You deserve the right to have more influence over others. You are better than they are."

Religious pride can arise when the focus becomes diligently following the right rules and traditions, rather than following Jesus. This not only hurts your own faith, but can be a huge turn-off for potential new believers who are repulsed by legalistic religion and its associated pride.

Pride of Comparison

Many pride-filled men continually compare themselves with others. They manufacture feelings of worthiness and superiority as they find others who are not as good as them in one thing or another. The pride of comparison leads to a life of judging others, looking for ways to show yourself and others how you might be better than the next person. This mentality leads you in the opposite direction as God's victorious game plan of focusing life on loving others and finding strength through God's power.

Pride Born out of Fear

Could it be that many times when pride shows up it's not really because a man truly feels so good about himself? Might much of the pride we display actually be a way to artificially boost our own ego because we fear we are not significant... that we don't measure up? Is at least some of our pride rooted in a need to project an image that's stronger, more in control, more significant, more successful and more masculine than perhaps we deep down really believe we are?

The Need to Level Pride

Every man struggles with several forms of pride. You can never completely eliminate *M.Y. Pride* from the game. He will continue to get in on tackles. If your team does not find a way to block Him, you'll always end up short. You will have major impediments to believing and loving God, because:

- you won't see your need for God;
- you will exalt yourself at the expense of God;
- you will be judgmental of others;
- your life will not center on serving and loving God and others;
- you won't seek help in prayer or accountability to others;
- you won't seek reconciliation for your sin; and

- you will maintain control and not allow God to work in you and through you.

Life loses proper perspective when pride interferes with putting God first. We cannot have peace. We cannot have rest in our souls. At a minimum, pride hinders faith. In many cases, pride is truly a faith killer.

Hall of fame Bears linebacker Mike Singletary wrote of the importance of setting aside his pride. He noted that after being broken and humbled and at the end of himself, he stopped running away from God and instead ran to Him. At that point he opened himself to God working in his life.[38]

The Solution to Pride

God knows how lethal pride is for most everything to do with faith, love and obedience to His will. He had to personally come onto the field and help you with this thug.

Jesus made God's position on pride crystal clear by repeatedly denouncing the prideful and affirming the humble. Jesus told story after story attacking pride, including this one:

> "Two men went up to the Temple to pray, one a Pharisee, and the other was a tax collector. The Pharisee stood by himself and prayed: 'God, I thank you that I am not like other people – robbers, evildoers, adulterers – or even this tax collector. I fast twice a week, and I give you a tenth of all I get.' But the tax collector stood at a distance. He would not even look up to heaven, but beat his chest and said, 'God, have mercy on me, a sinner.' I tell you this man, rather than the other, went home justified before God. For all those who exalt themselves will be humbled, and those who humble themselves will be exalted" (Luke 18:10-14).

Jesus came to block *Pride* by helping you: a) understand your true worth, b) live in humility, c) surrender to God, d) hold a servant's heart, and e) keep your eyes on the cross. The solution to pride is found in all of this… it's found in following Jesus.

Your True Worth

For so many men, our identity is entangled in an artificial image we create about ourselves to boost our own self-worth. When our self-worth is rooted in how much we do, what we own, and how we compare to others, prideful attitudes will be prominent. Knowing God's view of our worth can change these prideful tendencies.

The Bible says, "For we are God's masterpiece. He has created us anew in Christ Jesus, so we can do the good things he planned for us long ago" (Ephesians 2:10 NLT). We are God's workmanship, His masterpiece, His handiwork. Our worth is not wrapped up in what we do or what other people think of us. It's all about Who made us. God made us as His beloved work of art… each one of us.

The psalmist writes:

> "For you created my inmost being; you knit me together in my mother's womb. I praise you because I am fearfully and wonderfully made; Your works are wonderful, I know that full well" (Psalm 139:13-14).

You are a wonderfully made masterpiece… no matter what others see you as… no matter what you see yourself as… no matter what job you hold or how much money you make… no matter how many times you have failed… no matter how good you are at sports… no matter how many women you attract… no matter how physically weak or strong you are… no matter what vehicle you drive. The God of the universe wonderfully made you.

Jesus came to help you see your worth in God's eyes. We are valued so much by God that he left the bliss of heaven to come enter our broken world and lives. He came to be with us and personally touch the hurting. Jesus gives you your identity as a beloved child of God who is worth coming for and dying for.

Followers of Jesus no longer need to perform for anyone. They don't have to try and convince themselves or others how good they are. They accept themselves for who they are – created masterpieces dependent on the One who made them. Jesus referred to such meek people who understand their position with God as the "poor in spirit." "Blessed are the poor in spirit, for theirs is the kingdom of heaven," said Jesus (Matthew 5:3). The meek and humble know that they are weak and helpless and impure compared to God's strength and power and holiness. Yet at the same time Jesus gives them an inner confidence, because they know that their souls are treasured immensely by God. Their true identity rests in knowing Who made them and Who values them.

Living in Humility

The whole Bible directs us away from pride and into humility. One of many verses about humility in the Book of Proverbs reads, "When pride comes, then comes disgrace, but with humility comes wisdom" (Proverbs 11:2). God emphasizes the importance of humility when He declares in the book of Micah what He asks of us. "This is what he requires of you: to do what is right, to love mercy, and to walk humbly with your God" (Micah 6:8 NLT).

Some of the NFL's best players understand the importance of humility. Future hall of fame Quarterback Aaron Rodgers states in *Sports Spectrum Magazine*, "I think in the Kingdom, humility is God's favorite attribute. You have to have people in your life who keep you humble."[39]

LaDainian Tomlinson, who at the time of his retirement was fifth in career NFL rushing yards, is known for his humility.

LaDainian starts his day on his knees in prayer. "What I've noticed about him is through all the success he's had, all the financial blessings, the guy has never changed," said former Chargers defensive lineman and teammate DeQuincy Scott.[40] Drew Brees said of LaDainian Tomlinson, "LT is probably one of the most humble guys you'll ever be around."[41]

Another NFL player known for his humility was Lions running back Barry Sanders. After each touchdown run, Sanders quietly flipped the ball to the official and ran back to the sideline. On the final game of his rookie season, he needed 11 more yards to gain the NFL rushing title. Barry declined his coach's offer to go into the game with a few minutes left and gain the rushing title. In a subsequent season when he exceeded 2000 rushing yards, he refused to accept the game ball until his linemen were with him.[42] Sanders retired in the prime of his career, needing only 1457 yards to break Walter Payton's NFL career rushing record.

The humble recognize their need for our Holy and Sovereign God and they relinquish control to Him. A commonly used clarification about humility is: "Humility is not thinking less of yourself, it's thinking of yourself less." Humility is a life focused outward on God and the needs of others without reporting back to yourself about how good and helpful you have been.

Some misunderstand what it means to be humble. A humble man is not a human mouse with a low sense of worth. The meek and humble are not weak, but have tremendous inner strength. W. Philip Keller clarifies:

> "Meek men are not weak men. . . . they refuse to shove, push and throw their weight around. They do not win their wars with brutal battles and fierce fights. They win their way into a hundred hearts and homes with the passport of a lowly, loving spirit. Their unique genius is their gentleness. This quality of life does not come from a position of feeble impotence, but rather from a

tremendous inner strength and serenity. Only the strong, stable spirit can afford to be gentle. This quality is much more than a thin veneer of proper propriety or superficial politeness… Rather it is the epitome of a laid-down life, poured out, laid out, lived on behalf of others."[43]

While maintaining a gentle and loving spirit, a humble man can be both faithful and aggressive. Meekness is strength under control. Coach Vince Lombardi connected meekness with mental toughness, noting that meekness is the sign of true strength.[44]

The inner strength and courage of the meek man finds no need to look down on others or make something of other's weaknesses. He does not concern himself with what others think of him, and he sees no need to impress anyone. Combining humility and respect for others, meek men lift others by making them feel valued.

Jesus came and showed his followers how to live humbly. He did not look down on those in society who were sneered at by others, including adulterers, tax collectors, prostitutes, handicapped people, women, and children. Instead he approached them with love and compassion.

Jesus' humble demeanor attracted children. While Jesus' disciples thought Jesus should be spending time with those considered more important, Jesus called little children to Him and said:

> "Let the little children come to me and do not hinder them, for the kingdom of God belongs to such as these. Truly I tell you, anyone who will not receive the kingdom of God like a little child will never enter it" (Luke 18:16-17).

A meek man approaches God with childlike candor and vulnerability. In innocence and humility, he runs to God and trustingly jumps up in His arms.

Surrendering to God's Will

Jesus had the power to do anything. Yet for the first thirty years of His life we have no evidence that He used those powers. He showed complete restraint from the prideful temptations to use His power. He followed God the Father's will regarding the right time to begin using His powers.

As Jesus prepares for his public ministry, He hears from Satan's player *Pride* while in an extremely weakened physical state in the desert (see Luke chapter 4). "Demonstrate your power… turn this stone into bread… jump from this high point and fly," tempts Satan. "Deal with me and I'll give you plenty of authority, power and control." *Pride* comes to Jesus and hits Him with one temptation after another. And how does Jesus respond? He refuses the bait Satan offers. At every point He turns to the Word of God in Old Testament scripture. Jesus taught us to keep God's Word in our hearts and minds so that God's will dominates over our inherent prideful tendencies.

Jesus' entire life modeled a surrendering to the will of God the Father. Even at the end of His life, when contemplating the brutal death He was about to endure, He said, "Yet I want your will to be done, not mine" (Luke 22:42b NLT).

Surrendering to God is fundamental to faith. *Pride* is defeated when we surrender our life, choices, words, attitudes and actions to the One who so beautifully made us. Surrendering "is a lifestyle of enjoying God, loving Him, and giving ourselves to be used for His purposes," concludes Rick Warren, author of *The Purpose Driven Life*. Warren adds, "When we don't realize how much God loves us, we want to control our lives, and we misunderstand the meaning of surrender."[45] Surrendering has at its essence trust… being vulnerable enough to release control, let God love you, and then follow Him.

Quarterback Tim Tebow learned from his parents to submit everything in his life to God. His mom taught him to give all his disappointments and all his victories to the Lord. He noted that surrendering everything to God enables him to remain humble in success and lifted after defeats.[46]

Seahawks quarterback Matt Hasselbeck endured periods of failing as a quarterback, getting booed by fans and benched. In those times he humbled himself to be completely obedient to the will of his coaches, doing everything he was told to do and how he was told to do it, without questioning. "He came under the authority of others, and it's very difficult for a star player to have that kind of humility," said Jim Zorn, the Seahawks quarterback coach. "Matt did that. I think as a Christian, he knows how to come under the submission of the Lord, and that's something that translates to life."[47]

A Servant Heart

Emphasizing the importance of being a servant-leader, Jesus said:

> "You know that the rulers of the world lord it over their people, and officials flaunt their authority over those under them. But among you it will be different. Whoever wants to be a leader among you must be your servant, and whoever wants to be first among you must become your slave" (Matthew 20:25-27 NLT).

Jesus said about Himself, "Just as the Son of Man did not come to be served, but to serve" (Matthew 20:28a). One thing that sets Christian leadership apart from many other leadership styles is the idea of being a servant. Christian leadership is giving your best without having to be first. A follower of Jesus doesn't try to demonstrate his strength through his own superiority. Instead, he brings out the strengths of others through his own attitude of servitude.

One of Jesus' last acts was getting down on His knees and washing his disciples' filthy sandaled feet. Washing the feet of another was an act of lowly servitude. Jesus stooped down to wash the disciples' feet Himself to teach an important lesson (see John 13:1-16). John writes:

> "When He had finished washing their feet, he put on his clothes and returned to his place. 'Do you understand what I have done for you?' he asked them. You call me 'Teacher' and 'Lord,' and rightly so, for that is what I am. Now that I, your Lord and Teacher, have washed your feet, you also should wash one another's feet. I have set you an example that you should do as I have done for you" (John 13:12-15).

Jesus left His disciples with a lasting reminder of the importance of humble service to others. He was not ashamed to humble Himself as a servant. He spent His life serving and helping others. Jesus gave up home, personal comforts and time, to lead a life of healing, teaching, and caring for the needs of humanity.

The Bible says: "In your relationships with one another, have the same mindset as Christ Jesus: Who, being in very nature God, did not consider equality with God something to be used to his own advantage; rather he made himself nothing by taking the very nature of a servant" (Philippians 2: 5-7a).

Jesus on the Cross

Jesus' final act of selfless service was dying on the cross. When you comprehend what Jesus did for you on the cross, dying for your flawed self, your indebtedness crumbles your pride. He came for us and died for us. His amazing grace humbles us.

Humbled at the cross of Jesus, you cannot feel superior to anyone. You have nothing to prove to anyone. There is no room for pride, only gratefulness. You're ready to seek and conform to the God who is, rather than the God you want. Without

Pride's interference, you're in a position to love, honor and obey Him – ahead of yourself. You're willing to serve God and those around you.

Following Jesus destroys *Pride's* dominance. We know Whose masterpiece we are. We know God considers us worthy of coming for and dying for. When we follow Jesus, we see and feel His humility, His heart of servitude, His surrender to the will of the Father, and His trip to the cross of Calvary. Following Jesus leads us to a place of strength and confidence through meekness and humility. Jesus takes away our need to create impressions about our goodness and self-importance. It doesn't mean that *Pride* won't be in on tackles now and then. No one can constantly avoid pride. But *M.Y. Pride* will no longer be such a barrier to God and to victory. And by following Jesus, *M.Y. Pride* will be largely disabled from stirring attitudes of judgmental superiority.

Everything for victory we find in following Jesus Christ, including a heart that changes to trustingly surrender its pride to God. Following Jesus takes you where you want to go; and more importantly it takes you where God wants you to go.

 2nd down and 12 from your own 36. On a trap-run, M.Y. Pride is trap-blocked by your Lead Blocker who lined up as your offensive tackle and comes from the left side. Your Lead Blocker hits Pride so hard that He lifts him off both feet, clearing the way for you to pick up 6 yards before being tackled by the defensive end Barry N. Grave. 3rd down and 6 from your 42.

* * *

Huddle questions for Chapter 6 small group discussion are found free online at www.UltimateScoringDrive.com

Chapter 7

Conquering "Grave"

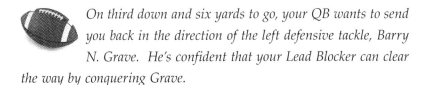

On third down and six yards to go, your QB wants to send you back in the direction of the left defensive tackle, Barry N. Grave. He's confident that your Lead Blocker can clear the way by conquering Grave.

An Eternal Question

Super bowl winning quarterback Trent Dilfer gained new perspective on life after his five-year old son, Trevin, passed away from heart disease. "If the motivation for your faith is what's going on in the 75 or 90 years we have on earth, then you are missing the truth of God's promises," noted Dilfer in the book *Men of Sunday*. "What God promises is eternity. This is not our home. When we make the decision to trust in Him and follow Him, our home is with Him for eternity."[48] "The take away for me," adds Dilfer, "is that so many things that we put a tremendous value on while we are here on earth pale in comparison to the eternal value of our souls. . . . There is tremendous value in what we do with our time here. But it is all a backdrop to our eternal lives. I get it now."[49]

The kind of eternal perspective held by Dilfer is foundational to a victorious life. Many do not trust that the essence of who we are, our souls, can personally enter into an eternity with God following death. Even many Christians do not consider the topic much, possibly having their own doubts and uncertainties, or perhaps they are just caught up in the immediate concerns of life.

On the other side of the line of scrimmage, the defensive tackle *Barry N. Grave* wants you unsure and disinterested in the topic of life beyond the grave. *Barry* knows that a diminished consideration or belief in an afterlife with God dampens both how we relate to God and how we live out our faith.

"Why even try to get to know God?" says *Barry N. Grave.* "If you do, it is just a temporary deal. Everything is severed when you die. You will be buried in a grave and rot."

Without an awareness of our heavenly afterlife with God, we are left questioning God's love for us and the importance of our relationship with Him. Could we really believe that God deeply loves us, if our all-powerful God keeps us away from His presence after we die? Yet if we can be assured God loves us so much that He's willing to bring our souls into His heavenly home with Him, our life and our relationship with God take on a whole new meaning. With confidence in heaven, we know our investment in faith is going to last beyond death. Our friendship built with God won't suddenly end. It will carry forward eternally.

An eternal perspective helps us to love and trust God even through our toughest life circumstances. We realize that God's big picture view of life holds a lot more than our comparatively short-term trials on earth. We can keep hope and joy alive, even during life's hardest times. An eternal perspective allows our choices, decisions, attitudes, values, priorities, money and relationships to all be viewed in light of a life transcending our brief moment on earth.

Tony Dungy is another man who, like Dilfer, holds an eternal perspective. He writes in *Quiet Strength* about how his job of coaching in the playoffs and Super Bowl was of minor importance compared to matters of eternal significance. Dungy used His abilities as a coach to reach the goal of winning a Super Bowl, but he never lost sight that his real purpose extended way beyond that football goal… reaching far into eternity.[50]

Souls Transcend Earth

The human soul crosses the threshold between this world and the next. Nothing else does. Statues crumble, and buildings and bridges collapse. But souls are forever. Our God of eternity is much more concerned about that which has eternal ramifications than He is about our immediate comforts. Our continuous comfort here on earth is not the ultimate goal as God sees it. God came as Jesus to teach us that life is not about growing comforts, but about transforming hearts and souls. And He came to give us confidence in the reality of eternal life.

Jesus remarked, "What good will it be for someone to gain the whole world, yet forfeit their soul?" (Matthew 16:26a). This game of life prepares us for the more important games ahead. Jesus said,

> "Do not store up for yourselves treasures on earth, where moth and vermin destroy, and where thieves break in and steal. But store up for yourselves treasures in heaven, where moths and vermin do not destroy, and where thieves do not break in and steal. For where your treasure is, there your heart will be also" (Matthew 6:19-21).

Jesus taught that we are to live this life as part of a continuum going from this life to the next. He said He would be preparing a place for us in heaven, and that He would come back and take us to be with Him (see John 14:2-3). Jesus repeatedly emphasized the relative unimportance of our creature comforts in this world compared to the vastly more important afterlife (see Mark 8:36-37, Luke 14:12-22, Matthew 5:10-12).

Jesus said "Do not work for food that spoils, but for food that endures to eternal life, which the Son of Man will give you" (John 6:27a). Soon thereafter Jesus declared:

"I am the bread of life. Whoever comes to me will never go hungry, and whoever believes in me will never be thirsty" (John 6:35).

Jesus' followers receive this food that endures to eternal life. But Jesus' followers are not so consumed with thoughts of eternity that they are lost and unengaged in this life. Christians who serve God and others to take action in this current life are those who clearly see life as a continuum between earth and heaven.

God wants you to live life to the fullest while on earth, and to have confidence that what you do here has a bearing on souls – souls that last into eternity.

How Can You Be so Sure?

An agitated *Barry N. Grave* shouts, "How can you be so sure of the reality of life beyond the grave? Do you also believe in fairy tales? An afterlife in heaven is just wishful thinking for those who can't face up to the harsh realities of this world."

Jesus came to bury the rhetoric of *Barry N. Grave* by giving us confidence about life beyond the grave. He not only taught us about the importance of everlasting life, He demonstrated its reality by restoring life to at least three people during his earthly ministry. Then in His most incredible validation of the reality of eternity, He returned to life Himself after dying on the Roman cross.

We can believe in our own eternity because of God's promises to us about an afterlife *and* because of Jesus' own resurrection from the dead. Jesus' return from the grave changed His disciples... and the world was never the same. Jesus conquered death and He promises to take His followers with Him to heaven.

The Bible places so much importance on Jesus' return to life after death that it says, "If Christ has not been raised, your faith is futile" (1 Corinthians 15:17a). Belief in Jesus' resurrection is critical for victory. And yet we sometimes can't help but question such a miracle.

It's normal to have moments of doubt. We get to the line of scrimmage and begin to question whether we can believe everything we read in our Playbook and were taught by our teammates.

God understands. Yet He absolutely does not want you to remain confused and unsure about something so important as life after death. God is not a God of confusion, but of peace (see 1 Cor. 14:33). God did not leave only verbal accounts of His life with us and His resurrection from the dead. He gave us both His Spirit and His written Word to support us in our beliefs.

You can't run an offense without a quarterback, and you can't have faith without the Holy Spirit. The Holy Spirit gives a peace about the truth of Jesus' life, death and resurrection to humble people who read the Bible with an open heart. In matters concerning faith and the spiritual dimension, God's Holy Spirit enlightens us and gives us an inner assurance about the truth of Jesus' teachings, His resurrection, heaven and eternity.

God supplements our Spirit-based convictions with reasoning. Reasoning can further strengthen our beliefs, as we look at the evidence and historical facts surrounding the Bible. *Barry N. Grave* would like to have people think that faith is divorced from intellectual reasoning. But a study of the Holy Bible shows a revelation of truth that is highly and uniquely supported. Reasoning clearly undergirds what the Christian knows is true through life experience and the voice of the Holy Spirit. Yet a person who stays in the intellectual frame of mind completely, blocking out the Spirit of God, will end up still unsure.

Volumes of books have been written on the subject of evidence supporting the truth of the Bible, including the truth of Jesus' rising from the dead. One notable author, Josh McDowell, was an agnostic college student who set out to disprove Christianity.

But instead, his research on the Bible led him to personally believe in the truth of the Biblical accounts of Jesus' life, death and resurrection. McDowell's subsequent writings include such books as: "Evidence that demands a Verdict," "More than a Carpenter," and "A Ready Defense."

Another author, Lee Strobel, was an atheist journalist whose wife's conversion to Christianity prompted him to thoroughly investigate the evidence concerning Jesus. After interviewing both believers and non-believers and studying the Bible, Strobel was so convinced of the truth about Jesus that he wrote books such as, "The Case for Faith," and "The Case for Christ" and "The Case for the Real Jesus."

McDowell and Strobel came to realize that the Bible writings about Jesus are largely based on written testimonies of the people who gave up their lives for what they witnessed and knew to be true. We have these testimonies not just from one witness, but from several.

They Saw Him Risen from the Dead

Jesus' disciples risked and gave everything, including their lives, to tell others of the resurrection. They had such boldness and confidence after seeing Jesus' return to life that they held back nothing - traveling, preaching, and writing in the face of life-threatening hostility. These men felt compelled to let others know that Jesus is God in the flesh Who rose from the grave.

God must have known that something so amazing as rising from the dead would be doubted throughout the centuries. He made sure to provide enough written testimony from eyewitnesses and friends of eyewitnesses so that humble truth-seekers can be confident in the reality of this event.

In the NFL, when there is a question about what happened on the field, the referees and audience can review the play from many different angles. With the Bible, we have written recordings to review the events of Jesus life, death and resurrection from several different angles. Each witness describes their experience through a different field of view.

The New Testament writings are a collection of documents written by several people, witnesses and close friends of witnesses, each testifying to Jesus' resurrection at a time when their lives were at great peril for even mentioning such a thing.

John is one key witness. He was a fisherman who became a close friend and disciple of Jesus. He wrote about Jesus' life, death and resurrection in great detail in the Gospel of John, emphasizing the divinity of Jesus and the way to eternal life through Him. John's other writings in the Bible include four letters written to individuals and churches. John was with Jesus throughout his ministry, on Calvary when Jesus was crucified, at the empty tomb, and with Peter and the other disciples when Jesus returned to life.

Peter, also a fisherman and disciple of Jesus, is another key witness. Peter's relationship with Jesus is described in each of the Gospels - Matthew, Mark, Luke and John. Peter's influence in starting the Christian church is described in the New Testament book *Acts of the Apostles*. Peter was imprisoned numerous times and was willing to die for the cause of spreading the word about Jesus. Peter exchanged his secure life of fishing, for a life of hardship, risk, ridicule, imprisonment and death, all because he knew the truth about Jesus being the Son of God who rose from the grave. Peter wrote that God "has given us new birth into a living hope through the resurrection of Jesus Christ from the dead" (1 Peter 1:3b).

Christianity spread because Jesus' disciples were transformed by Jesus and His resurrection. Ordinary fishermen became bold proclaimers of Jesus' divinity.

The evidence of Jesus and His resurrection is reinforced further with the witness of the apostle Paul. Paul did not see the resurrected Jesus in the days immediately following Jesus' death.

As a Jewish leader, Paul persecuted Jesus' followers, putting some to death. Then, Paul dramatically changed from a direct enemy of Jesus' followers to a staunch believer in Jesus. The first key event that changed Paul was when Jesus spoke to him from heaven during a trip Paul was taking to Damascus. Paul was blinded by God during this experience, and his eyesight was later restored by a follower of Jesus in Damascus. Paul later met with the disciples and eyewitnesses of Jesus' resurrection.

Paul's travels to spread the news about Jesus are well-documented in *Acts of the Apostles*. Paul did not write *Acts of the Apostles*, but he did write many letters included in the Bible's New Testament. Paul wrote concerning Jesus, "He was shown to be the son of God when He was raised from the dead by the power of the Holy Spirit" (Romans 1:4a NLT). Writing a letter to the Church at Corinth (about 15 to 20 years after Jesus' resurrection), Paul stated that Jesus appeared after the resurrection to "more than 500 of his followers at one time, most of whom are still alive" (1 Corinthians 15:6). In over 20 places throughout multiple letters, Paul specifically wrote about Jesus raised from the dead.

Paul gave up a very comfortable, secure, respected life and position within the Jewish church to live a life on the road and in prison, as he was tortured, repeatedly flogged and beaten with rods, stoned, shipwrecked, snake bitten, short of food and warmth, and despised by many. Eventually he was beheaded. He endured all of this because he was in a position to know the truth about Jesus' resurrection.

Paul's physician and traveling companion Luke, was a very learned man, and his writings include accurate details of names, dates, cultural facts, historical events, and the customs and opinions of the times during and immediately following Jesus' life. The *Gospel of Luke* and the *Acts of the Apostles* were written by Luke to accurately record the events of Jesus' life and how the disciples and others spread the word about Jesus after the resurrection. Luke knew the truth about Jesus from those who saw Jesus returned to life. Luke writes about Jesus in Acts 1:3, "During the forty days after his crucifixion, he appeared to the apostles from time to time, and he proved to them in many ways that he was actually alive."

The other Gospels of Matthew and Mark provide additional substantiation of the writings of others concerning the divinity of Jesus. Both books include accounts of Jesus coming back from the dead to meet with and talk to His disciples. For example, Matthew's narrative describes the angel's words at the empty tomb where Jesus' dead body was placed. The angel said, "I know you are looking for Jesus, who was crucified. He isn't here! He is risen from the dead, just as he said would happen. Come, see where his body was lying" (Matthew 28:5-6 NLT).

If Jesus had not risen from the grave, the disciples would have quickly gone back to fishing. There would be no Christian faith. But instead, the Church sprang to life. Many had not only experienced the living God in the flesh, they saw Him returned from the grave.

Recorded Accurately

Barry N. Grave, entering the picture again, retorts, "How can you have confidence in all those writings about Jesus' resurrection? How can you believe in anything written down thousands of years ago? Those are just ancient myths."

Grave's remarks sway many. But the facts reveal that the Jews were experts at accurate copying. The Dead Sea manuscripts, which represent copies of the Old Testament made during the first century AD, are virtually identical to corresponding texts written during the ninth century, which again are nearly identical to our Bible today. God, working through the scribes, made sure that scripture was copied accurately. Comparing the various copies shows that 99.5% of the New Testament is textually pure.[51]

Bible scribes wrote everything as was given to them, even information that the apostles, early evangelists, Gospel writers, text copiers, and those who assembled the Bible would have concealed, had they not simply been trying to report the events with the highest degree of integrity. For example, if they were willing to compromise integrity, they probably would have skipped copying passages reporting that women were witnesses of Jesus' empty tomb and resurrection. At that time and place, women were assigned such low societal status that their testimony was not admissible evidence in court.

If the objective was anything other than recording the truth, the Bible assemblers and copiers would have likely modified the New Testament writings showing the apostles as being petty, jealous, slow to understand, cowardly, and who either actively or passively failed Jesus repeatedly. The New Testament records embarrassing and confusing stories, such as disagreements between Apostles, and statements by Jesus that don't appear on the surface to make sense.

The stories were written and copied as they were remembered and shared. Those who told the stories and wrote them had everything to lose and little to gain by being truthful. They had experienced life with God in the flesh and nothing was going to stop them from spreading the entire truth.

Partial drafts or written collections of things Jesus said or did were likely in circulation for years prior to their use in the Bible's Gospels. Eyewitnesses of the events in question were still alive when Christianity was beginning and the Gospels were written. Most New Testament writings have been dated between 15 and 70 years after Jesus' resurrection.

You can have confidence that the words in the Bible today are what was written shortly after Jesus' life on earth. We have found 5800 New Testament manuscripts or fragments of manuscripts written in the original Greek language, an additional 10,000 in

Latin and over 9,000 in other ancient languages.[52] No other body of ancient literature in the world even comes close to having so many copies which allow textual comparisons.

God made sure the written accounts of Jesus' life, death and resurrection were recorded by several eyewitnesses and friends of witnesses, and that these writings were accurately copied over the centuries.

Following the Resurrected One

Many lives have been dramatically transformed by the risen Lord, Jesus. Their lives and testimonies show us the power of God through Jesus.

God gives us a lot of reasons to believe. Yet God does not just want us to have an intellectual belief in Jesus' life, death and resurrection. He wants us to hold a personal belief in which we receive Jesus personally into our life through the power of the Holy Spirit. A personal belief will lead us to truly follow the resurrected One – following Him on earth and eventually into heaven.

Jesus said, "For God so loved the world that he gave his one and only son, that whoever believes in him shall not perish but have eternal life" (John 3:16). When we follow Jesus, we don't just know Him during our brief moment on earth. We get to enjoy Him forever. God loves us so much that He wants us with Him in heaven. He is preparing our souls and the souls of our teammates for eternity in His presence. You can know that the relationship you build with Him now will not be severed at death, but will continue.

But Jesus did not say we *deserve* heaven or are entitled to it. In fact, Jesus said, "Not everyone who says to me 'Lord, Lord' will enter the kingdom of heaven" (Matthew 7:21a). Jesus repeatedly made it clear that not everyone will end up in heaven (see also John 6:40, Matthew 10:28 and Matthew 25:31-46). Rather we know from the Bible it is by God's love and grace and mercy that His followers will be raised with Him into heaven. It is a gift – one that we don't merit.

Follow Jesus from the cross of Calvary down the field to the empty grave and know the reality of eternity and the way to eternal life. Everything we need for victory in this life and the next we find in following Jesus Christ. Follow Jesus and you can have faith that your soul, your relationship with God, and the impact you have on the souls of others will all last into eternity.

An eternal perspective gained through Jesus frees you from the losing strategy of continuously satisfying your immediate earthly comforts and desires. Jesus is with you on the field to transform your life from one of expecting immediate feel-better moments, to one of constant hope and perseverance regardless of your current situation. The Bible says:

> "For our light and momentary troubles are achieving for us an eternal glory that far outweighs them all. So we fix our eyes not on what is seen, but on what is unseen, since what is seen is temporary, but what is unseen is eternal" (2 Corinthians 4:17-18).

When you follow Jesus, your earthly body will be buried, but you will be raised to life again in heaven. *Grave* is conquered. You live in the victory of hope, joy, freedom and perseverance, understanding the relative brevity of this life compared to eternity. You hold an eternal perspective that shapes your relationship with God, your heart transformation and how you reach out to the souls of others.

 3ʳᵈ and 6 from your own 42. On a run up the middle, your Lead Blocker positioned as your fullback clears the way for you, taking Grave completely out of the picture. You follow

right behind, picking up 7 yards before being tackled by the imposing force Cliff Impure. First down on your 49-yard line.

* * *

Huddle questions for Chapter 7 small group discussion are found free online at www.UltimateScoringDrive.com

Chapter 8

Nailing "Impure"

1ˢᵗ and 10 from your own 49-yard line. Still a bit dazed by the hit placed on you by Cliff Impure, you are only half alert when you come back to the huddle. Mistakenly thinking your QB called for a run to the right, you head the wrong way with the ball, only to be tackled for a loss of 2. Impure was right there to crush you again.

2ⁿᵈ and 12 from your 47. Your QB calls for a short pass to you. You roll right. Your QB throws the ball your way, but the ball is slightly tipped by Impure. You lose focus on the ball and drop it as it hits your chest. Incomplete. 3ʳᵈ and 12.

3ʳᵈ and 12 from your 47. Referee calls you for illegal motion. 5-yard penalty. 3ʳᵈ and 17 from your 42.

Exposed by a Bright Light

God is complete purity. The Bible says, "God is light; in him there is no darkness at all" (1 John 1:5b). Seahawks running back Shaun Alexander (NFL MVP in 2005) notes:

> "The goodness of God is foundational to all other teaching. Understanding that concept, believing it, and having it ingrained deep in your mind, heart, soul and spirit are essential for the walk of faith."[53]

God is the essence of love and purity, a light so bright we are blinded by His radiance. God detests darkness and impurity. Any bit of deceit, dishonesty, sexual lusting, mean thoughts, unconcern for others, cheating, disrespect, greed, malicious hurting, unrighteous anger, racism.... all of it is incredibly repulsive to God. Because God is so Holy, He cannot have companionship with sin.

Sitting in the stands at an NFL football game, the fans around you display much of the behavior God detests. If you watch a game on TV, the commercials appeal to the darker side of life... greed, envy, lust, and laziness. We live in a broken world, and we need not look any further than ourselves to see impurity and sin.

The defensive lineman *Cliff Impure* knows what sin does to a person when left unreconciled. He wants to use your impure thoughts and actions to maintain a cliff of separation between you and God, stopping all progress down the field. *Cliff Impure* is a superstar for the Spoilers.

There is no way you can reach the end zone without dealing with *Impure*. You can't avoid him by running right, left or up the middle. He will even block passes thrown to you. Not a single person can avoid *Impure*. He grabs your jersey as he encourages you to entertain wrongful thoughts. Then he throws you to the ground when your sinful thoughts lead to wrongful actions.

Impure's Lies

Even though *Impure* is a lineman, his range is anywhere on the field. Everyone can hear *Cliff* bellowing, "If it feels good do it! It isn't really wrong. God meant that commandment for some other culture, person or period of time. Self-control is overrated. You can't resist your natural callings...why even try... it just makes life boring." Impure adds, "You're better than most people... you have room to compromise a few values. Everyone else is doing it. They aren't giving it up, and neither should you."

Assisted by many of his fans who try to blur the lines of right and wrong, *Impure* first goes after your head, setting his cross-hairs on your thought-life. Everyone has tempting and impure thoughts from Satan's work, inherent impurity, and cultural influences. But *Cliff Impure* would like nothing more than to get you to invite, nurture and embrace your impure thoughts. Once you let your thought life get under his control, then the actions he wants will eventually follow.

Cliff Impure's biggest weapon for many men is sexual impurity. Our culture has plenty of allies for *Impure* in this area of our lives. "Porn will not affect you," lies *Impure*. Once you have stirred the lust of the flesh, *Impure* will try to convince you that it's too late. "You are beyond the point of returning to sexual purity."

We are never immune from the trial of remaining sexually pure. In fact, *Impure* may increase the sexual temptation heat when he sees you growing closer to God and effectively serving God.

Impure is an expert at leveraging wrongful thoughts into wrongful actions. Then he leverages minor indulgences into life patterns of sin and ultimately into major indulgences. Afterward he says, "You are the one who made that decision to do it. This is who you really are, someone who can't control himself. You are not worthy of God's love. Just stay away from Him."

A Debilitated Relationship with God

Good and evil coexist in every human heart. None of us can remain completely holy. The Bible says, "For all have sinned and fall short of the glory of God" (Romans 3:23). Similarly it says, "If we claim we are without sin, we deceive ourselves and the truth is not in us" (1 John 1:8).

Jesus, fully knowing that nobody can claim a sinless life, challenged a group of people who were condemning an adulteress, saying, "Let any one of you who is without sin be the first to throw a stone at her" (John 8:7). Everyone dropped their stones.

The question is not whether you have sin; you do. But are your patterns of choices leading you toward God and holiness, or pulling you further away from God? In subtle or obvious ways you are progressing in one direction or the other. The more you choose one direction, the harder it is to make choices in the other direction.

Your sin left unchecked eats away at your character, lowering your capacity for making pure and holy choices into the future. You become ensnared in a downward spiral that can be a quick slide or a very gradual almost unnoticed fade. Yet every time you choose good instead of sin, you are growing in the character of God's likeness. Every time you conquer a temptation, you become more like Jesus, and you have greater strength for making right choices into the future.

One thing is certain; nobody makes the right choice every time. *Cliff Impure*, who at first says "no worries... sin freely," is right there to use that sin to pull you away from God. Depending on your personality and background, *Impure* tries to lead you toward one or more of the following responses to your sin:

> *"Hide from God.* You should be ashamed of yourself. You are not worthy of God's presence. Hide from God, just like Adam did in the Garden of Eden after he disobeyed God."

> *"Avoid what convicts you.* You really don't want to feel convicted by your actions. If you just avoid God, you can avoid the weight of guilt – you can avoid what convicts you. Don't go to church, don't read the Bible, don't pray much, just stay away from anything holy that might lead you to those unpleasant feelings of conviction and guilt."

> *"Deny God.* Who says His standards are right and yours are wrong? You can easily defend your behavior. Just keep justifying your actions and maybe you can get that nasty conscience seared and numb to the voice of God."

> *"Work, baby, work.* You can regain your worthiness. Get to work trying to do good stuff, and more good stuff. Keep it up with the hope you will amass enough on your 'good list' to prove your worthiness of God's love."

"Rebel against God. Do whatever you please. It's time you let God know that you don't need his standards. There is no reason that you shouldn't let your self-pleasing behaviors reign freely."

"Ignore God. You are doing most of the right things. You should be proud of your own goodness. You don't really need God for anything. Just ignore Him."

Whether your impurities lead you to hide from God, avoid God, deny God, work to prove your worthiness, rebel against God, or ignore God, it all makes *Cliff Impure* smile. Your separation from God will not only thwart victory here on earth, but will have eternal consequences. One who has continued to make choices leading to further and further separation from God does not automatically construct a bridge across this chasm of separation after life is over. Our entirely pure, Holy and just God will not ignore our sin and impurity, bringing dirt and grime into heaven as if anything goes, as if nothing really needs to be reconciled, cleansed and made right.

God's Plan for Handling Impure

So how can we get past this separation from God on earth and in the afterlife caused by our impure and other sinful thoughts and actions? Like everything, the Followers Team Leader has a rock-solid plan for a victorious outcome. And like all His plans for destroying barriers to victory, it centers on Jesus.

Knowing Right from Wrong

God's plan is NOT to have you wander through life confused about what is right and wrong, not knowing what will bring you long-term blessings and what will bring you harm. God gave you certain commandments and directions in the Bible to help protect you from yourself, serving as beacons of light in a dark world. These laws include foundational principles of right and wrong, and principles for having a right and proper relationship with God. God also gives you an internal moral compass to help you apply the Bible to your daily life and discern right from wrong.

Recognizing the Sin Within

God's commandments were importantly given to help us recognize the towering height of the cliff separating His Holiness and our sin. The Bible says, "No one will be declared righteous in God's sight by the works of the law; rather, through the law we become conscious of our sin" (Romans 3:20). The law, God's commandments in the first five books of the Bible, provides a way for people to see their total inadequacy to abide by God's holy standards. They help you see your need for getting right with a Holy God, preparing your heart to yearn for God's grace.

Jesus took it a step further to help us see our failings. He taught that the divide between people and God is not just about wrongful actions, but also impure intentions of the heart. Jesus compared lust in the heart to adultery, and anger toward others to murder (see Matthew 5:21-22, 27-28). By doing so, he made it clear that our own internal attitudes and heart are known by God. God sees hidden sin in everyone… the hurting person and the happy person… the good person and the evil person.

Jesus confronted the self-righteous to help them see their sin residing deep within their heart (Mark 10:17-18). But He gave the good news of redemption from sin to those who already understood their sin and had a hunger and thirst for righteousness (see John 3:1-21 and Matthew 5:6). For both groups, God first wanted them to recognize their sin so they would turn to God for reconciliation.

The Need to Reconcile

God's plan is not to leave you alone with your bad choices, ignoring the fact that you're moving into more and more destructive behaviors which harm you in the long run and further distance you from God and His Holiness. The enemy considers it a Spoilers victory when you continue your normal patterns of sin.

God warns His people repeatedly about the consequences of sin. "For the wages of sin is death" (Romans 6:23). Impurity, left unreconciled, debilitates our relationship with God and stops the scoring drive. God does not want your sin to be a permanent chasm between you and Him. He wants your attention. He wants your heart… a heart that's full of love and full of Him. That can't happen when your sin remains unreconciled.

Come as You Are – Everyone!

God's plan is not to have you trudge through life with the unwieldy burden of guilt constantly on your shoulders. That's a joy-sucking way to live, opposite of what God wants for you.

Getting your life straightened out before you come to God is also certainly NOT a part of God's plan. Rather, it's all about getting right with God in spite of your sinful nature. God's plan has you coming to Him with all your impure thoughts and actions. You do not need to clean up your life in order to come to God. Hall of fame cornerback Deion Sanders discovered this, writing:

> "I was under the illusion that if I ever wanted to be a Christian I had to get my life straightened out first. I thought I had to do my own thing so I would be good enough for God to save. But what I eventually discovered was that you don't get yourself together to come to Christ. You come to Christ so you can get yourself together."[54]

God came to earth as Jesus to teach us we're never so lost that we can't come back to Him. God will always accept you right where you are, if you will only ask Him (see Luke 15:20-24).

Jesus also made it known that faith and God's love does not just belong to men of high societal standings or certain religious circles, as many thought at the time. It is for everyone – women, children, men, poor, unpopular, sinners, outcasts... anyone and everyone.

Bridging the Separation

The Bible makes it clear that the sacrifice Jesus made as He suffered and died on the cross was on behalf of our sin. Through the cross, God makes sure you know how serious sin is – so serious that it required an extreme remedy – God Himself dying in the most tortuous and public way. Through the cross, God showed you how much He loves you, willing to take on the harshest death to restore you and reconcile the unholy areas of your heart and life.

All penalties for your misgivings are covered on the Cross of Christ – they have been paid for in full. You can come to God freely. You don't need to prove yourself worthy of God's love. Because of the cross, followers of Christ are welcomed into heaven without further consequences for their sin. God wants us to accept with gratitude the grace and mercy He offers, to repent and turn away from our sin, and then recommit our life to Him.

The cliff of separation from God created by our impurities and all other sin were bridged by Jesus as he died on the cross for us.

- Through the cross, God makes it clear that you don't need to hide from Him after you sin. You can come running to Him for forgiveness.
- Through the cross, God makes it clear that you don't need to avoid feeling convicted of your sin. Your goal is not to avoid feelings of conviction, but rather come to Jesus

to repent and seek reconciliation, knowing He already paid the penalty.

- Through the cross, God makes it clear that the standards for right and wrong are not lessened whatsoever. You cannot deny God and His Holy standards, as the reconciliation for violating them come at a great cost.
- Through the cross, there is no room for pride, since you didn't do the hard work to reconcile the problem; Christ did it for you.
- Through the cross, you see the love God has for you. With His love in constant view, you will be more apt to turn from your impure ways. You'll be motivated by God's love for you more than a desire to avoid punishment.

The Bible says that God "rescued us from the dominion of darkness and brought us into the kingdom of the Son he loves, in whom we have redemption, the forgiveness of sins" (Colossians 1:13-14). God uses the cross of Christ to not only defeat *Impure*, but to also rescue us from all sin-based barriers to Him, including *Pride, Self, Passivity* and others.

God does the work on the cross to re-establish the fellowship with God that is separated by sin. As you repent of your impurity, God's forgiveness removes the great sin-obstacle to your relationship with Him. We know in our heart we are free to come to Him. We are forgiven. We are clean in God's eyes – as white as snow. "There is now no condemnation for those who are in Christ Jesus" (Romans 8:1).

Living in Freedom

As you humbly come to Jesus with your failings and turn your heart toward Him and follow Him, you are set free. God's plan not only frees you from self-destruction, guilt and penalties, but it frees you from living with a legalistic focus on a set of rules. God's way lets you live in freedom (see John 8:31-36). You're led not by your willpower to follow rules, but by the power of the Holy Spirit to follow Jesus.

If a football team spent most of their energies thinking about what rules to follow and penalties to avoid, the game wouldn't be much fun and the team wouldn't make much progress. Instead, the successful teams go out on the field inspired by their coach and team leaders and their vision for victory. They are aware of the rules, but they play with heart and they play with freedom.

The more you focus on what behaviors to avoid, the more you think about those impure things, which can then draw you into those behaviors. The way to turn from your wrongful ways toward greater purity and holiness is not to focus on what *not* to do. Instead, the answer lies with giving yourself completely to being with the sinless Jesus; to follow His words, His life, and His righteousness. This approach allows you to play in this game of life with heart and freedom.

Through Jesus, we know we are loved, forgiven, and adopted into God's family now and into eternity. A heart-felt recognition of this makes us want to obey God and become more like the sinless Jesus. In love and gratitude, we obey.

God of the First Down

When you mess up on the football field, you often have chances to redeem yourself. You have four downs to keep the drive alive. Penalties and mistakes on the first two or three downs won't end the drive. Because of your mistakes on first or second down, you may have more ground to make up, but you're not necessarily done. Make it to the first down marker and the drive continues with a whole new set of downs.

Nobody who has ever played your position has done it perfectly. Even after we surrender our life to God and follow Jesus, we still mess up. We lose sight of the game plan. We don't listen so well to God's Word and our Quarterback. We don't follow Jesus so closely. We may get called for illegal motion or false starts.

Thankfully, God is the God of the first down. While God does not limit us to four downs, the beauty of driving down the field with Jesus is that you can start anew after veering off-course. You can rebound from your mistakes, get the first down, and keep the drive alive. You can head back in the right direction with the ball firmly in your grip. In the scoring drive of life, we all need multiple first downs.

The key to getting first downs is repentance – remorsefully turning away from your failings, and turning back to following Jesus. Recognize where you messed up, confess it to God, give it to Him, and allow the Holy Spirit to renew you from within. Claim the cleansing that God offers. Accept God's grace and forgiveness. First down – press on.

Super Bowl winning quarterback Trent Dilfer needed a first down, and he got one. As reported in *Sports Spectrum Magazine*, Dilfer admitted to getting caught up in a life where his actions and attitude were separating him from God. He was living for himself in his night-life, while at the same time mixing in some church attendance and Christian meetings. Dilfer realized he needed help, and he turned to God's love and the forgiveness Jesus offers those who turn from their ways and turn to him. Dilfer's life changed for the better as he began living for God. He got the first down. Yet that didn't mean he wouldn't need other first downs. Dilfer stated:

> "I'm a big-time work in progress. I spend a lot of time on my knees asking God to change me. Anytime you ask God to change you, He will answer you and it's often painful. It has been very difficult at times. The reward has been well worth the struggle, because as I see God change me I see Him start to mold me into somebody He can use."[55]

We all are big-time works in progress. We all need multiple times of letting God change us and mold us. We all need fresh starts.

Fresh Starts

An NFL quarterback who needed a fresh start in a big way was Michael Vick. During Vick's NFL years, he neglected the Christian faith introduced to him by his grandmother. He slipped into a life of living only for himself. "The only person I cared about was me," wrote Vick in his autobiography *Finally Free*.[56] Vick ended up in prison due to his major involvement with dog fighting rings.

Vick's 21 months in prison brought him back to Jesus. In his cell-room bunk he began reading the Bible every night, just as he had in high school. God was the only One Vick could reach out to during many days and nights in prison. Vick remained hopeful that as he trusted and believed, God would give him a fresh start.

Vick followed Jesus and listened to the repeated encouragement of Followers teammates like Tony Dungy. God gave Vick a new beginning. God gave him a chance to show others that if you obey God, work hard, and remain humble and accountable, a guy can bounce back after falling hard.

Released from prison, Vick came back into the NFL and led the Eagles to the playoffs. Vick also set career highs in passing yards, passing percentage, QB rating, passing touchdowns, and rushing touchdowns. He was selected to his fourth Pro Bowl and named the NFL "Comeback Player of the Year."

You will also mess up on your drive down the field. We all do. Most of you won't end up in prison for your mistakes. But nonetheless, you will blow it in little and big ways. Thankfully, while God desires perfect execution of every play, He's going to keep you in the game even when you mess up. He hopes your continuing presence on the field, under the leadership of your

Quarterback and daily life with your Lead Blocker, will enable you to get back on track with a fresh start and maintain the march toward the end zone.

God does not want you to dwell on your past mistakes. You should *not* continue to condemn yourself over sins God has already forgiven. There should be no more worry, no more wondering if you are truly forgiven. This is only going to distract you from doing your job well on the current play. Once you have realized your mistakes and remorsefully turned to Jesus, you're coached to forget what is behind and strain toward God's pure light. Do not let *Cliff Impure* or anyone else hold you in bondage to historical sins.

God's grace in giving you a fresh start will draw you closer to Him. A growing closeness to God will lead you to increasingly despise anything in your own life that goes against God's will. You grow in trust and obedience, faith and worship, prayer and praise, submission and service.

Linemen Penetrated

Reconciliation of sin and impurities, and everything else needed for victory, is found by following the One who gave his life to reconcile our sin, Jesus Christ. You are forgiven through Him. You're free to come to Him and grow in your closeness to God.

At its core, Christianity is a willingness in the heart to follow Jesus… a willingness to trust and surrender to Him and live close to Him… to repent from our sin and turn to Him. As you do, *Cliff Impure* is nailed. Your fumbles, failures, impurities and sin are no longer barriers to God and heaven. Your old life is exchanged for a new life in Christ. With thankfulness in your heart, you desire to keep following Jesus down the field of life.

With the four linemen now taken care of, the heaviest hitting is done.

- You know God is active in your life. He loves you, values you, and wants you to know Him by following Jesus. *Isolated* is annihilated.
- Through knowing Jesus and following his ways, you have humbled yourself enough to seek God, surrender to Him, lean on Him and accept His help. *Pride* is leveled.
- You have confidence that life extends beyond this earth. Through the resurrection of Jesus, you have an eternal perspective that gives you a hope, freedom, and joy. You know that through the love of God your soul will transcend this life. *Grave* is conquered.
- Your separation from God caused by your impure heart, actions and self-centeredness has been reconciled with God through the sacrifice of Jesus on the cross. *Impure* has been nailed by the cross of Christ.

You are now a believer who has received God's love and Holy Spirit. You are following Jesus. Your soul is saved. You're experiencing the most substantial and freeing victory of your life.

As the clock continues running and you resume your march down the field, the Spoilers are not going to leave you alone. When you become a believer, the power of sin and death over you is defeated; but sin is not eliminated. The enemy still has several ways of oppressing you and steering you away from truly trusting God. The Spoilers have many ways to prevent or stifle your growth into a mature victorious believer who is all-in for God. Next you will be moving into linebacker territory… a place where you either learn to more fully trust God or otherwise live with fear, embitterment, disillusionment, and emptiness.

As a result of three mistakes on this set of downs, it is 3rd and 17 from your 42-yard line. Your Coach calls for a pass up the middle. As your Quarterback drops back to pass, Impure rushes in and nearly reaches your QB before your Lead Blocker collides with Him. The pass gets off and is well-thrown. This time you catch it securely and pick up 14. Fourth and 3 from your opponents 44.

The Followers decide to go for the first down with an off tackle run. You get the ball and follow right behind your Lead Blocker who crashes into Impure with a full head of steam, clearing the way for you to pick up just over 3 yards and a first down. You realize that without the block on Impure you would have been stopped cold and had to turn over the ball.

* * *

Huddle questions for Chapter 8 small group discussion are found free online at www.UltimateScoringDrive.com

Part III.
Through the
Linebackers - Trusting

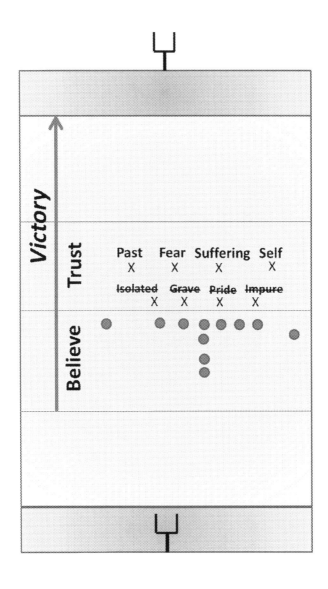

Chapter 9

Crushing "Suffering"

1st and 10 from the Spoiler's 41. Your QB drops back to pass. The Blitz is on. The team's Lead Blocker picks up the blitz and keeps the play alive. Your QB quickly tosses the ball to you. You jump high and make the catch at the Spoiler's 37-yard line. Hit hard while in mid-air, you twist your ankle upon landing. Teammates come to help you up. You realize that you cannot place much weight on your ankle without pain. Putting your arms around your Lead Blocker and another teammate, they help you off the field. You question why this happened at this time. "I was doing everything I was supposed to on the field and we were moving the ball," you think to yourself.

Watching from the sidelines, it's 2nd and 6 from your opponents 37-yard line. Your Quarterback steps back to pass. Someone misses their blocking assignment and you see your Quarterback sacked by the linebacker Ben Suffering. Loss of 6. 3rd and 12 from your opponent's 43-yard line. A timeout is called to assess the situation. In the meantime, your team trainer examines your ankle.

Injured

"I knew that every time I stepped onto the football field there was a chance that I could get hurt," said Jerry Rice[57]. Eventually Rice tore some major ligaments in his knee while tackled by his facemask. Hardships can happen to the best NFL players. No-one is immune. Tough players can end the season on any given play.

Many players get injuries that hurt tremendously; yet the type of injury allows them to keep the game and season alive. They gut it out with remarkable determination. Walter Payton broke the NFL single game rushing record while playing with a temperature exceeding 102 degrees and stomach sickness.[58] In Super Bowl XXVIII, Emmitt Smith carried the ball 32 times for 168 yards despite suffering a dislocated shoulder that he heard cracking throughout much of the game. Emmitt refused to stop playing. He gained 42 yards on a final drive to allow his Cowboys to kick the winning field goal.

Brett Favre is one of the most well-known players of iron will. Before Reggie White joined Favre on the Packers, he played against Favre. Reggie recalled:

> "I thought Brett could be something special, because I remembered the game we played against him in November 1992. I remembered hitting Brett so hard, his shoulder separated. I told myself, 'Okay, he's out.' But he came back. And threw for 275 yards. And two touchdowns. With a separated shoulder. And he beat us."[59]

Favre set an NFL record with 297 consecutive starts. He played with numerous injuries throughout his career, not letting his pains force him off the field. His injuries included: a separated shoulder, sprained ankles, sprained foot, fractured ankle, ankle bone spurs, sprained thumb, sprained hand, broken thumb, elbow tendinitis, elbow nerve injuries, sprained knee ligament, concussions, torn biceps, pulled groins, and a severely bruised hip, thigh and hamstrings. Finally in 2010 he was unable to start due to a shoulder injury in one game and a concussion in another game. Between 2003 and 2006 Favre played in the face of: the sudden death of his father, the death of his brother-in-law during an all-terrain accident on Favre's property, his wife's bout with breast cancer, and his boyhood and mother's home destroyed by Hurricane Katrina.

Most veterans inevitably play during times of severe pain and times of difficult personal circumstances. Pain and suffering are also inevitable for everyone playing on the field of life. You will get injured. It doesn't matter how well or how poorly you're playing, injuries and hardship can and will happen. The One in charge of the Followers doesn't promise that by playing on His team you will be free from troubles.

Life's Pain

Bad things happen. You may lose a job, need surgery, crash your car, lose a loved one, or suffer broken relationships. You may have kids who rebel. People may attack you by theft or assault. There are illnesses, depression, disappointments, heartaches, and failures. Sometimes we are blitzed with multiple afflictions at the same time and the pressures of life are mounting. We have to keep playing in this game of life while under great duress.

Not only do hard times come our way personally, but we see much of the world in a mess. History and current affairs show us that bloodshed and injustices occur beyond belief. We see innocent countries attacked, dead soldiers, holocausts, and devastations from hurricanes, tsunamis and tornados. Thousands die from nasty diseases. We are sickened as we learn of the mass suffering taking place in warlord ruled areas, in hospital emergency rooms, in inner city streets, in bullet strewn school rooms, and in earthquake zones.

We can make sense of some aspects of pain. When we think about why our bodies experience physical pain, that part of suffering makes some sense. Tony Dungy's son Jordan is missing a gene which allows a person to feel pain. Through Jordan, Dungy is keenly aware of how pain protects us, teaches us and causes us to change self-destructive behaviors. God uses all kinds of pain to protect us. Emotional pain can prompt us to pull away from destructive patterns. Physical pain lets us know when something is wrong in our body that needs attention.

We can make sense of injury and tragedy that happens when we choose to take part in sports and activities involving higher levels of risk. Some people die while hang-gliding, mountain climbing, swimming with sharks, race-car driving, motocross, or ski-jumping. Sometimes the odds just catch up with higher risk activities.

We can also make at least some sense of tragedy naturally stemming from disobedience to God. Suffering arises out of the free choices God allows people to make. Both evil and love results from our free will. God could not program our every decision to be loving, or else love loses all meaning. It must be a free choice. A world that allows for true love from the heart cannot operate in any other way. People are given the freedom to individually choose love or evil, purity or sin, right or wrong.

Many bad things stem from people choosing the path of disobedience to God. Pornographic infidelity leads to disrespect for women and can ultimately lead to divorce and split families. Hunger for power can lead to wars and death of loved ones. Lies lead to more and bigger lies which lead to hurting others. Drug addictions can lead to crime and imprisonment. Neglectful parenting can lead to teenage crises. Alcohol abuse can lead to physical and mental abuse and deadly accidents. Gluttony can lead to heart attacks. Greed of some leads to starvation of others….. and on and on.

While we can generally understand why a body experiences pain and why free-will is necessary, there is still so much that we really can't fathom. Why cancer for this good person? Why this innocent person's life? Why that tornado hit here? Why that killer's brain went haywire? Why this baby died before she was born? Why that tire blew? Why that beloved person is so susceptible to addictions? Why God intervened to stop this tragedy and that problem, but not this other one? Why that genocide did not stop sooner than it did? We can't understand.

In some cases we can scratch our head till we bleed and still not grasp why a certain specific bad thing happened. Some situations are so appalling that our heart burns and our mind swims, grasping for any glimpse of understanding. And that understanding just cannot be found. We often can't help but ask "why?" We often can't help from being angered.

B.S. Suffering Says, "There Can't be a Good God"

Then you hear the words of the enemy linebacker *Ben Suffering* ("B.S." for short). "So you've been suffering, have you? Of course you have! That's because God doesn't really care about you or the rest of humanity." B.S. aims to highlight these bad things and then leverage suffering to steer you away from God. He can be enormously distracting, bellowing while your Quarterback is preparing to take the snap. *Suffering*'s first aim is to create doubt in your mind that God really even exists. He moves up to become a 5th man on the belief-stopping defensive line and shouts:

> "Why would He allow good people to suffer and be killed? How could God allow a child to die from disease? He's not really active in this world. C'mon… look at this world full of chaos, destruction, and pain. God can't really be here. Not on this planet."

If he can't get you to release your belief in a God who is involved in this world, his second aim is to get you to lose trust in God. He steps back into his linebacker position and tries to convince you that you can't trust this God of yours:

> "With all the bad in this world, how can you say your God is loving or caring? There is simply too much suffering for anyone to believe in a good God who loves people. Don't you see it? God is uncaring! He has forgotten humanity and you just can't trust him."

B.S. sometimes uses hard times and evil to make you believe that God is against you personally:

> "Look at what has happened to you... God is either angry with you or against you. If he loved you he would make life smoother. God is certainly not looking out for your best interest."

Some listen to *B.S.'s* arguments and decide to give up on God. "After all," they argue, "*Suffering* makes a good point." "I know of plenty of bad things that have happened to people. I can't explain them. God doesn't seem to care. Maybe He's not even there." Some reach the saddest point of all, telling themselves, "If there is a God and He allows this kind of suffering, I don't want any part of Him."

Others refuse to listen to *B.S.'s* rhetoric, fully believing in God's love. They may have a time of being angry with God, but they know God well enough to trust Him as they walk on a narrow bridge over some awful stuff.

How do you personally react to the words of *Ben Suffering*? Where do you turn when you see lives of others in an upheaval, or when your own life turns to tragedy? Does it drive a wedge between you and God or does it drive you closer to God? Does *B.S.* leave you crushed on the turf, or are you able to get up and huddle with your teammates again?

Jesus Leads the Way

Jesus acknowledges the difficulties of life. He said, "In this world you will have trouble" (from John 16:33). Jesus was not sent here to explain away suffering. He was not sent here to take away all adversity. But He did come to change hearts for the good, and as a consequence reduce the amount of evil and resulting suffering. Jesus knew that suffering would always remain a part of the human condition.

God comes onto the field of life as Jesus to help get us through our trials, and in the process strengthen our faith, character and compassion for others. When we follow Jesus, we see that:

- Pain and tragedy come to good people too;
- God understands the depth of our pain;
- God cares about our pains - He has a heart for the hurting and stays with us through our suffering;
- Death is not the end of the story; and
- God makes some good come out of life's troubles and hardships.

Jesus helps us get through our difficulties without letting *Ben Suffering* get the best of us and our faith. God does not provide the reason for each experience of pain; and we still need to trust through much of what we can't understand. But through Jesus, He provides the means to face suffering with hope, rather than bitterness and despair.

Pain and Tragedy Come to "Good" People

Jesus was the most morally upright person who ever lived, yet He had to endure plenty of pain. Through Jesus we know that hard times in life are not reserved for those who have moral failings. Jesus not only dispels this myth by his own life example, but he addresses it verbally when he was asked about whose sin caused a man's blindness (see John 9:1-3). Jesus answers that neither the blind man's sins nor the sins of his parents caused the blindness. He adds that it happened so the work of God might be displayed in his life.

God does not promise a life free from pain and hardship, even if you're trying to live a pure and holy life. You and other good people you love will experience hardship and tragedy. You will get injured. You can count on it.

Godly people are not immune from ill treatment. Christians around the world face tribulation, persecution, imprisonment, famine, peril and sword. Jesus knew this would happen. He did not say God would stop all harm from happening to such faithful people. He said, "If they persecuted me, they will persecute you also" (John 15:20). He said that you're going to have hard times.

The apostle Paul was beaten and whipped on several occasions, was shipwrecked three times, and imprisoned for long periods (see 2 Corinthians 11:23-28). He was hungry, thirsty, mistreated, and persecuted. He survived stoning and eventually was beheaded. He knew that the blood of Jesus was not shed simply to make our lives trouble-free. If escaping adversity was the goal, Paul would have shouted through a megaphone, "Don't come my way." On the contrary, he encouraged people to come to Jesus as he did.

Another persecuted faithful man during Jesus' time on earth was John the Baptist. The Bible says that John the Baptist was the greatest man born to a woman; yet he ended up in prison and was then beheaded. We question, "God, how could you let that happen to such a good person?"

Often God saves us from awful situations; but sometimes He chooses not to. Through the life of Jesus, John the Baptist, the apostle Paul, and many others in the Bible, you can know that "good" people are not immune from suffering.

Jesus states, "In this world you will have trouble." More importantly, He adds, "...but take heart, for I have overcome the world" (John 16:33). Tony Dungy concludes, "That's how we have to handle it - by letting Christ handle it. We may not be able to handle all the adversity, but Christ who lives within you definitely can."[60]

God Understands – He Experienced It

One thing you can be assured of... God understands your pain and suffering. He has been there. Jesus experienced many of the bad things that happen to people.

- God understands mockery, because He has been mocked;
- God understands being hated and rejected, because He was hated and rejected by many;
- God understands death of loved ones, because He experienced a close friend's death;
- God understands evil governments, because He lived under the Roman occupation;
- God understands being treated unfairly, because He was unjustly persecuted;
- God understands physical pain, because He was viciously flogged and nailed onto a cross;
- God understands abandonment, because He was abandoned by even His friends;
- God understands imprisonment, because He was jailed;
- God understands homelessness, because He lived without a home; and
- God understands dying, because He died on the cross.

In Jesus Christ, God experienced the greatest depths of pain. If God allowed Himself to go through these things during His time on earth, you can know that the bad things happening to you are not because God doesn't love you. It's not because God is detached from the human condition. God hurts with you as you experience a world of pain and suffering.

God Cares Deeply for the Hurting

God came to earth as Jesus to show us just how much compassion He has for the suffering. Jesus was side-by-side with the hurting. He spent considerable time lifting the spirits of the downtrodden, healing the sick, and casting demons out of mentally unstable people.

Jesus typically took the extra step to not only heal the hurting, but to connect with them personally. He listened intently to them, talked to them and placed His hands on the hurting. Even those with leprosy, He touched! The hand and heart of God reached out to touch people who others would not touch. Jesus showed us how much God does care. He's truly with you, especially during your times of pain.

God invites you to come to Him during the hard times. He loves you and hears your cries. He stays with you in your despair and is a source of peace, comfort and strength. Jesus said, "Come to me, all you who are weary and burdened, and I will give you rest" (Matthew 11:28).

This Short Life Compared to Eternity

So much of tragedy involves death - death of loved ones and death of the innocent around the world. God came to us as Jesus to help us through one of life's greatest pains - the sting we feel when loved ones die and the ache we experience when we learn of others who died or are dying.

We can maintain hope through Jesus' promises of life after death and the reassurance He provided through His own resurrection from the dead. We have hope that the death of those we love and our own death will be an entry point to a permanent home of love and surpassing beauty. We will be reunited with the souls of loved ones in a place without suffering. God reassures us that this life is not the end. Death in all its pain is not the last word. The hope of eternal life does not remove the sadness of losing a loved one, but it can help us get through such sorrowful times.

If this life is everything, then it becomes much harder to trust God in a world of diseases and natural disasters. But Jesus helps us see this life as a blip in time compared to eternity. This eternal perspective makes it easier to trust that God knows what He's doing when He does not continuously intervene to prevent horrible happenings.

God Creates Good out of Tragedy

The Bible says, "We know that in all things God works together for the good of those who love him, who have been called according to His purpose" (Romans 8:28). God will be able to make something good in the bigger scheme come out of every bad situation involving His followers. We can't always see it. But it is there. It still doesn't explain suffering or justify painful experiences or console our personal tragedy. But Jesus' followers can trust God to bring good in the face of suffering as He works through His faithful people.

The Bible is full of examples where people intended things for evil and God used them for good. Joseph in the Old Testament is a prime example. He was sold into slavery by his brothers and later unjustly imprisoned. Yet these hardships resulted in God being able to use him for saving a large population from starvation.

Tony Dungy lost his son Jamie from suicide. Losing a son or daughter to suicide must be one of the hardest things anyone can ever experience. Dungy's faith and words surrounding his son's passing helped many others whose families have been impacted by suicide. By Dungy remaining so faithful in such painful circumstances, the message of hope through Christ was loudly proclaimed.

Quarterback Randall Cunningham also knows the pain of losing a child. His 2 ½ year old son Christian drowned in their backyard hot tub. In his book *Lay it Down – how letting go brings out your best*, Cunningham discusses the importance of his faith and supportive friends and family in getting through such pain. After experiencing a number of tough times in his life, Cunningham concludes:

> "It's not that bad things happen in the face of a good God and He does nothing. It's that even through the worst of calamities, God can bring about beauty because He is so good."[61]

God "brings about beauty" through troubling times. He uses compassionate responses by some people to open hearts in others. He will use difficult times to help believers grow in character, grow closer to God, and more fully transform their hearts into Christ's likeness. Sometimes God will take a hardship and use it to wake up a man to faith - a faith that will help him tremendously throughout the rest of his life and lead him to heaven.

Awakened to Compassion

Philip Yancy writes:

> "When God shouts to us through suffering and pain, it has a haunting effect. It's much harder to believe the world is here just so I can party when a third of people go to bed starving each night."[62]

Clearly, our experiences in this world are not all about how much fun, care-free living we can pack into our years. Life is about showing, giving and receiving love. When people step forward in compassion to help and support those who are suffering, there is a great potential for their own heart to grow. And when the afflicted feel such love from others, their heart can grow as well.

Faithful people showed up to help Aaron Smith (defensive end for the Steelers) get through some tough times. Smith tore his bicep in 2007. In 2008 his son Elijah was diagnosed with leukemia. In 2009 Smith tore his rotator cuff, and in 2010 his season ended with a mid-foot sprain. He said, "My faith has grown tenfold during this process. . . The community is so important, a small group who supports you." [63]

God came to earth as Jesus to show us how to love the hurting. Jesus leads us to take care of the poor, visit the prisoners, feed the hungry, take care of the sick, and give to those who need clothes or drink or the necessities of life. As we follow Jesus in this way, love will surround the suffering, and hearts will grow, including our own. The power of God's grace will be revealed to others who see how you compassionately respond to the broken world around you.

Awakened to Faith

Quarterback Kurt Warner was personally close to his wife's parents, who were both killed in a tornado soon after they retired. Warner's faith had been very gradually evolving in the months before the tragedy. Warner wrote in his book *All Things Possible* how this tragedy drew him closer to God than ever before.[64]

"Sooner or later everyone is driven to prayer," notes Randall Cunningham. "That's what life does; it moves us toward God."[65]

In his book *Wild at Heart*, John Eldredge concludes, "Until we are broken, our life will be self-centered, self-reliant, our strength will be our own. So long as you think you're really something in and of yourself, what will you need God for?"[66]

While not everyone may need to be broken by major hardship before they walk humbly with God, that's the case for many. Our injuries, pain and suffering wake us up and get us to look beyond our self, to look up, and to see the eyes of God looking down on us. God will often take a tragedy and use it to draw people closer to Him and therein lead them to find the source of all love and strength.

Many people would prefer to avoid the topic of God altogether, feeling comfortably numb and apathetic to faith. But when death takes the life of someone they love, or when the world starts to crumble before their feet in divorce, job loss, or news of cancer, all of a sudden the question of Jesus' resurrection has more relevance. God will be there at these waking moments to make His presence known. He will often bring His followers onto the scene to help the afflicted through their challenges and help them know about God's love for them.

Vikings Pro-Bowl safety Karl Kassulke was in a motorcycle accident during the height of his NFL career. The accident left him paralyzed and in a wheelchair. Kassulke poignantly wrote about his life prior to and following the accident in the book *Kassulke – true story of Minnesota Vikings star Karl Kassulke & the accident that changed his life – for good.* Kassulke concluded:

> "Obviously, I didn't think that I needed that motorcycle accident. But that was what it took to bring me to my knees. I don't think I ever would have done it otherwise. . . . I have learned something that I wouldn't trade for all the money and fame in the world. I've learned that knowing the Lord is everything. And without the Lord, there just isn't anything solid to hang on to in this world. . . . I enjoy my life immensely, even more than I did when I was walking. My life is filled with love and joy, and I am finally at peace with myself."[67]

Over time, Karl was able to see how God worked through his tragedy to create a better outcome – a faith that brought joy in this life and that set him up to live with God eternally.

Even the faithful need periodic wake-up calls. Super Bowl winning Quarterback Trent Dilfer reflected on how God used tough times in his career to teach him how to more fully trust in Him, stating:

> "I'm not afraid to say that early in my career I wasn't real mature. I think many times you have to go through adversity and hard times for God to change your life. It took a lot of heartache for God to get through to me and to build those characteristics in my life." Dilfer adds, "It was during the rough times I stopped trusting in myself and learned to lean on God the most. I recognized His power and His ability to carry me through circumstances that I'm not comfortable with."[68]

Drew Brees observes, "Many people would define the 'good life' as one that's free of pain and hardship and heartache." But it was an ACL injury in high school that caused Brees to question and reflect on life's deeper meaning. It was during his recovery that the "light bulb came on" for him, an "epiphany" leading him to trust God and develop a relationship with Him. The recovery period was a life-defining time that made him stronger mentally, physically, and spiritually. Brees wrote, "That injury was the best thing that could have happened to me."[69]

One way God makes good come out of bad is by using hard times to wake us up to a better life… a victorious life in truly following Him.

Building Character

God places us on a field where we are sometimes hit pretty hard. The Bible says, "We can rejoice, too, when we run into problems and trials, for we know that they help us develop endurance. And endurance develops strength of character, and character strengthens our confident hope of salvation" (Romans 5:3-4 NLT). God will use some ugly circumstances to help His children grow in faith, strength, character and joy.

Most of us are not too quick to sign up for the character-building crash-course. But we also don't hear that people learned their most profound lessons in life and grew closest to God during their fun, easy, sunny days. Many people admit at some point in their life that much of what they really needed for long-lasting joy came to them through their most difficult and painful experiences. Some look back on an illness or injury and recognize that it was an irreplaceable season of personal and spiritual growth.

Reggie White noted, "The greatest blessings I've ever experienced are the hard times. . . . During our hard times Sara and I have learned obedience, learned to depend totally on God."[70] This statement is repeated often within and outside the NFL.

Eagle's defensive lineman Jerome McDougle almost died after getting shot in the gut at point blank range while being robbed. McDougle said, "Going through that experience made me stronger in my faith and in Him, because it put me in a position where I had to trust in God."[71]

Following Jesus through Suffering

Life has its warm sunlit days and its bone-chilling blizzards. Periods of glee are followed by periods of great sorrow. God gives us the power and peace to stand tall amidst it all.

Jesus said that when you build your life on the solid rock foundation of God and follow Him, you will be able to weather the major storms in life (see Matthew 7:24-27). He didn't say the storms would not come. You will have trouble. Anticipate it. Prepare for it. So that when you're knocked silly by the hard hits in life, you're prepared to reach up your hand and allow Jesus to pull you back onto your feet. He will not only help you up, but will make you stronger from the hits and more compassionate for those who get hit in the same way.

Jesus shows us how we can overcome the world... how we can turn to God in our pain. He reminded people time and time again that this life on earth is not our final home. Earth is not heaven. We can have a blessed assurance with Jesus Christ that our eternity will be spent in heaven.

Jesus shows us the love and compassion God has for the hurting. We know through Jesus' life that God can relate to anything we go through. He promises to be with us always, and He will especially stay with us as we go through tough times.

How will you respond when you get "injured?" Randall Cunningham shares some godly wisdom:

> "When we go through a trial in life, we tend to search for a way out of it. But we often don't realize that the solution is right in front of us. God promises that he will

never leave us or abandon us. If we can remember this truth when we experience the friction that life brings, then we will not allow anger or bitterness or despair to overtake us."[72]

By following Jesus as He heads in *Ben Suffering's* direction, you can trust Him to clear the way so that this adversary does not stop your progress down the field. It's not that you will avoid the hits in life by following Him, but you can still maintain progress down the field.

Mark Brunell, NFL quarterback for 19 years, has worked through many difficulties in his life. He concluded, "When you put Jesus before every decision, every thought and every action, things will be ok. . . . I think the Christian life is boiled down to two things: you obey and you trust."[73]

By trusting and obeying Jesus, the apostle Paul was able to keep joy and peace through his difficult times. He writes, "We are hard pressed on every side, but not crushed; perplexed but not in despair; persecuted, but not abandoned; struck down, but not destroyed" (2 Corinthians 4:8-9).

Everything we need for victory we find in following our Lead Blocker, Jesus. By following Him and leaning on Him, hardships and pain will move you into a closer relationship with God. God may use your tough times to change your heart - to become stronger, more merciful and more compassionate. You'll be better equipped to help others get through their trials. Your heart will grow. And others may see the love and compassion in your heart and seek the same kind of peace you have with the same God of the universe. By following Jesus, hardships will help bring victory. The rhetoric of *B.S.* will be drowned out by the voice of God's truth.

The timeout provided you with just enough time for the trainer to confirm that you only have a slight sprain. Your ankle is quickly wrapped. As you get up and place some weight on it you can tell you don't have the strength in that leg you had earlier. Coach asks you if you're ready to go back into the game. You are hurting, but you want back in. You run back into the huddle. Your QB calls a draw play. He drops back as if to pass while your Lead Blocker heads downfield to take Ben Suffering out of the play. The ball is handed to you. You shoot a large gap and cut left toward the place where Suffering lays on the turf. After a nice gain, the fearsome linebacker Max Fear cuts you off. Fearing the hit he's going to deliver, you duck out of bounds just two yards shy of the first down. 10 yard gain. 4th and 2 from the Spoilers 33.

* * *

Huddle questions for Chapter 9 small group discussion are found free online at www.UltimateScoringDrive.com

Chapter 10

Flattening "Fear"

Several of your teammates noticed that your fear of Max Fear caused you to step out of bounds two yards shy of the first down. In the huddle they encourage you to take courage and go right back in the direction of Max.

Crippled by Fear

Lists of the all-time most feared NFL tacklers include players such as: Jack Tatum, Lawrence Taylor, Dick Butkus, Steve Atwater, Ray Lewis, Jack Lambert, Ronnie Lott, and Joe Greene. But offensive players usually fear some other things more than hard-hitting defensemen. Many football players fear mistakes, failing, and losing. They fear what their coaches, teammates, fans and the media might think of them. They fear being cut from the team.

Related fears crop up on the field of life. We often fear failure, rejection by others, and vulnerability. Each can be impediments to victory. In combination, they can cripple faith.

As men, we typically don't like to admit we have fears, or worse yet admit that parts of our life are controlled by fears. We fear we might look weak to others if they know we fear. Yet underlying fears cause many of our negative thoughts, stresses, anxieties, insecurities, and worries.

Max Fear wants to magnify our fears so we play the game with anxiety, timidity, and distraction. Satan's team masterfully uses fear to stop us, bind us and rob us of the joy of playing the game. *Fear* can speak so loudly that God's voice is drowned out. If *Max Fear* can get you to constantly worry about one thing or another, he knows his team will gain a major advantage. Your energies will be diverted away from serving God and others.

Fear looks for allies like depression or sleep deprivation, which he uses to further intensify worries and blow things completely out of proportion. He will use the dark of night to engulf the light of a Holy perspective.

Max Fear's goal is to at least handicap your faith, if not cripple it. He wants you consumed by fearing bad things that could happen; and your energies then spent making contingencies to avoid those fears from becoming a reality. *Fear* wants you to keep your eyes on the circumstances of the fear, and off of God. "Fear strangles everything that faith has given you," notes Seahawks running back Shaun Alexander.[74]

God tells His people over 100 times in the Bible not to fear. He speaks through the Old Testament saying, "Be strong and courageous. Do not be afraid; do not be discouraged, for the Lord your God will be with you wherever you go" (Joshua 1:9). Isaiah pens the words from God, "So do not fear, for I am with you. Do not be dismayed for I am your God" (Isaiah 41:10a).

It's not realistic to think we can completely eliminate all fear. Even 49ers hall of fame quarterback Joe Montana, known for his coolness under pressure, admitted to having pregame jitters. He said that most players get nervous, even the stars.[75] Yet Montana was able to convert his fears into motivation, maintaining great poise amidst turmoil on the field.

We won't ever have a life where fears and stress do not creep in. That's a good thing. Temporary fears and stresses prompt us to take necessary or helpful action, such as protecting our self and others. Sometimes fears lead us to seek God and His power and peace. Sometimes they can help wake us up to what is truly important in life, such as our eternal destination.

Jesus said a certain kind of fear can help non-believers. He said, "Do not be afraid of those who kill the body but cannot kill the soul. Rather, be afraid of the One who can destroy both soul and body in hell" (Matthew 10:28). God doesn't intend Jesus' words to paralyze believers with fear, but instead to wake up the sleeping.

While temporary fears can sometimes be a good thing, patterns of recurring fears, worries, anxieties and stresses only distract us, steal joy and eat away at faith. They stop us from fulfilling God's callings for our lives. Patterns of fear hinder our relationship with God and obstruct the Holy Spirit's work to transform our heart.

Jesus wants to be your lead blocker Who flattens *Max Fear* and ensures that distracting, joy-sucking, trust-hindering fears do not take hold of you.

Trust

Jesus says, "Do not let your heart be troubled. You have put your trust in God. Put your trust in me also" (John 14:1 NLV). Trusting in God foils *Max Fear*'s victory-debilitating impact. Since the level of trust depends on the character of the one you trust, it's important that you know God's character. The more you get to know His character, the more you will trust Him. The more you trust, the less fear takes hold of you.

We trust God because He is Holy. God's Holiness overarches all of His being. Nearly a thousand times the Bible states that God is Holy. It is intrinsically who He is. He's utterly distinct and set apart, incomparable, and so far above us that we can't comprehend His full glory. God's Holiness, His majesty and His infinite moral perfection and purity inspires awe and worship.

We can trust God because He is sovereign. He is all-powerful. That does not mean He's necessarily initiating and orchestrating every single thing that happens. But He is ultimately in control, ruling over every affair in the universe. From beginning to end, the Bible is replete with examples of God's sovereign power. You can turn to Jesus even in the darkest times, confidently knowing that He and His Father and His Spirit are ultimately in charge of the universe.

We can trust God because "God is love" (1 John 4:8 and 1 John 4:16b). The Bible says, "There is no fear in love, but perfect love drives out fear" (1 John 4:18b). Through Jesus, we see that God loves us so much that He was willing to step into our world's messes and die on the cross for us. When we start to realize how much God loves us, when we grasp that truth deep within our heart, *Fear* looses his grip on your jersey.

We can trust God because He is faithful and merciful. The Bible says, "Cast all your anxiety on Him, because He cares for you" (1 Peter 5:7). We can trust that God hears us and will be faithfully attentive when we call out to Him. Paul writes:

> "Do not be anxious about anything, but in every situation, by prayer and petition, with thanksgiving, present your requests to God. And the peace of God, which transcends all understanding, will guard your hearts and your minds in Christ Jesus" (Philippians 4:6-7).

The Bible does not say that God responds to every request the way we want. He is not a universe genie granting our every desire. But He's attentive to the pleas of our soul and He'll guard our "hearts and minds in Christ."

Jesus showed us what to do with our anguish and worries. During the one moment when Jesus seemed to fear, knowing He would be temporarily separated from God the Father while He took on the sins of the world, Jesus prayed. He prayed that God the Father's will would be done. He modeled how to trust the One who is attentive to our life and to our prayers.

When you get to know the character of God by spending time with Him, His Son and His Word, you will see a God of immense love, attentive faithfulness, and sovereign power. Because of His character, you can trust God through fears of failure, fears of financial and physical vulnerability, fears of other's opinions, and all other fears that tackle you.

Fear of Failure

Failure is such a scary word to most men that our lives are sometimes driven more by fear of failure than a desire to succeed.

Chuck Noll, who coached the Steelers to four Super Bowl victories, once reportedly said that one of the worst things that can happen to a person is to fear failure.[76] He did not want his teams to lose games because they went out on the field fearful about losing.

Fear of losing is one way our fear of failure rears its ugly head. We fear mistakes, being wrong, failures at work, financial ruin, letting others down, or just plain being a failure. *Max Fear* comes along to say, "Don't even try it... you are not good enough... you're just going to fail." We listen to *Max* and then avoid stepping in with courage to accept a challenge that would well serve God and others.

Other times *Fear* says, "Work like a dog just so you don't fail. It doesn't matter what the toll is to your faith, family or health... you just can't fail." Whether you avoid risks altogether or work like everything to avoid any chance of failure, either way *Max* is a happy linebacker. Both responses steal your peace. Both steal the kind of victory God desires for you.

The All-Pro center for the Indianapolis Colts, Jeff Saturday, is an exception to the masses of men who fear failure. "Whether I lose 7-62 or win 62-7, it's not going to change me. I'm going to be the same guy... my relationship with Christ is truly my identity. That's really all I am about," said Jeff in an interview for *Sports Spectrum Magazine*. Jeff Saturday continues:

> "I think the older I've gotten and the more success I've had, the more failures I had, I realize how limited I am as a person. . . . Whether it be a success or a failure, I give it all to Him. And God, take it, do whatever you want with it, and show me how weak I am as a person, but how strong I can be with you."[77]

People like Jeff Saturday do not fear weakness or failure because their identity is not caught up in their worldly success. They know their identity remains as a child of God – a wonderful created masterpiece made by the source of all life and love.

Tony Dungy is another man who has a godly perspective on failure. He writes in his book *Uncommon* about how failure is a normal part of life for everyone. He adds, "Success is really a journey of persistence and perseverance in spite of failure."[78]

Failures are part of the human experience. Jesus knew it well. Jesus' friend Peter failed Him on several occasions. One time Peter was invited by Jesus to walk on water over to Jesus. Peter followed Jesus' invitation, but began to sink when fear caused him to take his eyes off Jesus. Peter also failed by sleeping through a prayer meeting with Jesus in the Garden of Gethsemane. And after spending nearly three years at Jesus' side, three times Peter fearfully denied knowing the arrested Jesus.

In spite of his failures, Jesus does not give up on Peter. At one point Jesus tells him that on Peter He will build His church. After Jesus' resurrection, Jesus tells him again to follow Him and to feed His sheep. Peter was used in big ways to spread the Gospel and start the Christian Church. Jesus never gave up on Peter, and He won't give up on our failures. In essence he says, "Keep taking that ball and hitting the hole. Get up again and again, no matter how hard you're knocked down… I am not going to give up on you."

Instead of fearing failure, the Seahawks running back Shaun Alexander keeps the focus on doing everything to the best of his ability. Alexander writes,

> "I honestly believe that I'm supposed to do everything I can do to the best of my ability, and God takes care of the rest... How can you worry if your Father's taking care of everything? The God that created the world says, 'I got you; just give Me the best you got.'"[79]

God can use your failures when you learn and grow from them. He wants you to take risks for Him, knowing that you might fail. Just do your best, pray that it's blessed, and trust in His love and faithfulness for the rest.

Fear of Being Vulnerable

Men don't like vulnerability. We fear weakness. *Max Fear* has been working on us throughout our lives so that we fear financial, physical, and emotional vulnerability.

Financial Vulnerability

Men will often try to avoid vulnerability by building security through work, bank accounts and possessions. *Fear* says, "There is no place for peace in your life when the future could bring you financial disaster... Before you know it you could be out of money and unable to provide for your family."

Jesus comes into our life to say, "Do not worry about your life, what you will eat; or about your body, what you will wear. For life is more than food, and the body more than clothes. . . Who of you by worrying can add a single hour to your life?" (from Luke 12:22-25). Jesus reassures us that we are a lot more valuable to God than the birds that He feeds and the flowers He clothes with splendor. God does not want us to replace thoughts about His goodness with worries about financial security. Instead He calls us to wisely and generously use the money He gives us to help others and glorify God.

The Bible teaches that our real security does not lie in our bank account, but in our confidence that we are loved unconditionally by the Creator of everything. Jesus comes into our life to say, "Do not worry about tomorrow, for tomorrow will worry about itself" (Matthew 6:34a). Jesus asks that we trust in Him and surrender everything to Him, including our fears about financial vulnerability.

Jesus taught us to defeat by surrendering. Surrendering and giving control of your life to God releases worry and fear, replacing it with joy and peace.

Vulnerability of Aging and Death

Max Fear says, "You should never have peace, knowing that aging and death looms in your future."

We fear aging partly because we fear the vulnerability of losing control and depending on others. The thought of being laid up in a nursing home sends chills up our spine. In death we lose all control, as our soul and our eternal future are completely in the hands and mercy of God.

It's hard not to have at least some fear of death. After all it is a pretty big step… a major change from what we are used to. But God does not want His followers consumed by safety and mortality to the point where it interferes with our relationship with Him and the peace we bring to others.

Jesus releases our bondage to the fear of death. The Bible says, "…by his death he might break the power of him who holds the power of death – that is, the devil – and free those who all their lives were held in slavery by their fear of death" (Hebrews 2:14b-15). The promise of eternal life by Jesus and his own return to life after death gives us weaponry to fight the universal fears of aging and death.

You can trust that God is preparing your soul for eternity with each phase of life, including your most vulnerable senior years. Jesus says, "Whoever hears my word and believes him who sent me has eternal life and will not be judged but has crossed over from death to life" (John 5:24). At the end of our lives we can trust placing our soul into God's hands.

Reggie White, the hall of fame Packers defensive end, died unexpectedly at age 43. About a decade before his death he wrote,

"I know many people fear death, wondering what's in the next life and whether they will reach heaven. But I don't fear my own death because I know where I'm going. I don't fear the death of my children or my wife because I know where they're going."[80]

Reggie lived in peace, trusting in God's faithfulness to His promises of everlasting life.

Emotional Vulnerability

Another common fear for men is emotional vulnerability. It can threaten the image we portray of our manliness. A man's ego is all too often working to convince himself and others that he's strong no matter what is happening. We feel like we don't dare show weakness, sadness, depression, or anxiousness. Sometimes we might even avoid helping others through tough times, fearing that we may be placing ourselves in an emotionally vulnerable position.

Jesus showed us how we can be emotionally vulnerable and strong at the same time. A very short but profound verse in the Bible is, "Jesus wept" (John 11:35). Jesus placed Himself in one situation after another that tugged at his heart and emotions. He had no fear of emotional vulnerability.

The apostle Paul also placed himself in physically and emotionally vulnerable situations. He followed Jesus and fully trusted God. Paul noticed that through his weakness, he was being made stronger. He writes, "That is why, for Christ's sake, I delight in weaknesses, in insults, in hardships, in persecutions, in difficulties. For when I am weak, then I am strong" (2 Corinthians 12:10). By following Jesus, Paul lived in freedom from fearing vulnerability.

Fear of What Others Might Think

Former offensive lineman for the Broncos, Mark Schlereth, admitted that one of his fears in the NFL was getting his name announced by the stadium announcers.[81] Linemen don't usually get singled out for making a great block. When a lineman gets their name announced it's usually because they got called for something like holding.

Nobody likes the jeers of 60,000 disappointed fans. Nobody likes attention drawn to their mistakes or getting booed. But many of us not only fear boos, we fear any sort of disapproval, criticism, or rejection. We continually assess what others might think of us.

Max Fear shouts:

- "Don't share your faith. If you do, others may think you're a religious zealot."
- "Don't confront people, or others will think you're a 'know-it all.'"
- "Keep up every appearance of a man of faith, even if your faith has grown cold on the inside. You don't want people to think your faith is weak."
- "For heaven's sake, don't show up at a Bible study where you might feel small and humiliated by your lack of Biblical knowledge."
- "And keep away from close relationships where others might get to know your true identity."

Max Fear is so successful with this fear tactic that we often make our decisions and spend our words in an effort to manage the impressions others have about us. John Ortberg insightfully notes in his book *The Life You've Always Wanted,*

"Human conversation is largely an endless attempt to convince others that we are more assertive or clever or gentle or successful than they might think if we did not carefully educate them."[82]

We can't completely eliminate caring about what others think of us. But when casual consideration of others' opinions veers into a continuous reflection of what others might think, we are not following the game plan or our Lead Blocker.

Looking to Jesus, we see someone who never once feared what others would think of Him. He did not care in the least if others criticized Him, questioned Him or thought less of Him. He ate with tax collectors, spoke to prostitutes, and 'worked' on the Sabbath when those activities were shunned by most. Jesus was fine with saying things that caused others to turn away. He didn't soften His message or worry about his popularity. In fact, many turned away from Him based on the hard facts He told about the sacrifices needed to truly follow Him (see John 6:66).

Jesus' only concern was loving obedience to God the Father. Jesus lived in freedom… free to speak the truth in love… free from the need to create an impression. Everything about Jesus was authentic and genuine. When we follow Jesus, kneeling at His feet, we can live in the freedom of authenticity.

When Panthers wide receiver Steve Smith followed Jesus, he discovered freedom from the fear of vulnerability. After going through some very difficult times and then turning to God, Smith noted in an interview for *Sports Spectrum Magazine:*

"I've been encouraged as I've gotten older and Christ has gotten ahold of me to be vulnerable, to be transparent, to all people to see 'Hey, I am flawed, and I have made mistakes."[83]

Tony Dungy also lives in the freedom of authenticity. He wrote, "Somebody pointing out the limitations, real or otherwise, doesn't change my strengths or the truth that I am and will always remain a child of God."[84]

One other notable person who did not fear human judgment was the apostle Paul. He wrote:

> "I care very little if I am judged by you or by any human court; indeed, I do not even judge myself. My conscience is clear, but that does not make me innocent. It is the Lord who judges me" (1 Corinthians 4:3-4).

Max Fear is Flattened

Jesus said, "Peace I leave with you; my peace I give you. I do not give to you as the world gives. Do not let your hearts be troubled and do not be afraid" (John 14:27). As you follow Jesus:

- Fear of failure is replaced by a life of taking risks for God's glory;
- Fear of financial vulnerability is diminished by knowing that God is on the field with you and is bigger than any economic distress;
- Fear of aging and physical vulnerability is reduced through surrendering control to God and simply delighting in His presence;
- Fear of emotional vulnerability is diminished and largely replaced by the freedom to live authentically and genuinely;
- Fear of death is diminished by assurance of eternal life in heaven;
- The fear of what others think of you fades into a life centered on your audience of One – the Lord; and
- Timid tendencies are replaced with power, love and self-discipline to serve God and others (see 2 Timothy 1:7).

We will always have fears. And that's ok. Every situation invoking fear is also an opportunity to turn to God and prayerfully trust in Him more. But by following Jesus, *Max Fear* will not take you down. Instead, your fears will lead you to greater trust, greater faith and ultimately to victory. You can trust your holy, loving, faithful and all-powerful God through your fears.

Everything we need for victory we find in following Jesus Christ, including freedom from a life distracted and controlled by fears and worries. *Max Fear* is flattened as you follow Jesus.

4th and 2 from the Spoilers 33. After catching a quick pitch from your QB you head toward the outside following right behind your Lead Blocker. As Max Fear comes in to make the tackle, Fear is flattened. You pick up some yards and then start to lose focus, thinking about the likely press interviews and money that will come from your good work on the field. The linebacker M.T. Self tackles you after a gain of four. 1st and 10 from your opponents 29.

* * *

Huddle questions for Chapter 10 small group discussion are found free online at www.UltimateScoringDrive.com

Chapter 11

Smashing "Self"

You return to the huddle thinking about your future in football and how all your great playing is going to get you everything you ever wanted. Your teammates try and snap you out of your distraction and get your focus back on the rest of the team. They remind you that victory is not about personal statistics, gaining fame or finding fortune.

Two Big Drivers for Men

The thrill of winning the Super Bowl and being part of football history brings both euphoria and a sense of importance. The winners feel pleasure and some sense of significance.

On and off the field, the desires for pleasure and significance drive much of a man's life. We yearn for pleasure. Yet, the bigger driver, one of man's most innate needs, is significance. We need to be relevant - to have purpose and meaning.

How a man arrives at fulfilling both pleasure and significance will determine whether he's headed for victory or utter defeat.

How do you personally strive for pleasure and significance? Do you randomly stuff things into your days that bring a fleeting pleasure and a false sense of significance? Or do you intentionally seek out long-lasting joy and true significance?

M.T.'s Lure to Self-Absorption

On the opposition's defense stands the linebacker *M.T. Self*, who often goes by "*M.T.*." He's fully aware of your longing for pleasure and significance, and he has his own ideas of what you should cram into your life. "Indulge your own ambitions and desires with self-gratifying things and activities," he advises.

M.T. Self seems greatly interested in your well-being. "Look out for number one," he cries. "What you need to do is make sure you are happy. You come first." *M.T.* claims, "I have many things that can bring you pleasure and many things that can help you feel significant."

"You want pleasure... come into my store," invites *M.T.* You enter his shop to find boats, fast cars, electronic gismos, video games, recliners, big TVs, 4-wheelers, parties, beach towels, hot tubs, barbeque ribs, action movies, bottomless margaritas, and topless servers. "C'mon," says *M.T..* "Buy it, eat it, drive it, spend it, charge it, watch it, drink it, own it, seduce it. This is what life is all about... this is real pleasure!"

"I know you need some significance in your life too," says *M.T. Self.* "You need accomplishments, power, influence and prestige." He shows you some pictures. "You'll feel significant driving this big truck. You'll feel significant after climbing this mountain and running this race. You'll feel significant by building this business; hiring these people; sitting in this office; having these offspring; winning this game; breaking this record; building this large home; making these 'important' decisions; and having your picture on this wall."

Not all of what *M.T.* offers are bad in and of them self. But the entire focus, motivation and methods of finding pleasure and significance are part of a losing strategy. If you listen to *M.T.,* you will think your greatest investments must be in yourself. By following *Self,* your life will be enslaved by *my* pleasure, *my* desires, *my* entertainment, *my* accomplishments, *my* toys, *my* self-security, *my* self-comforts, *my, my, my.* Oh my – we have a real me-first mess in our culture. It is a mess that leads to emptiness and disillusionment.

Discovering the Lie

Deion Sanders came to realize that living for me-first pleasure and self-focused significance did not bring fulfillment. Sanders wrote:

"I remember winning the Super Bowl that year.... That same week I bought myself a brand new $275,000 Lamborghini and I hadn't even driven a mile before I realized, No, that's not it. That's not what I'm looking for. It's got to be something else. . . . I was running. I was hurting. I had plenty of money and everything else a man could want, but I was desperately empty inside."[85]

Karl Kassulke, the Vikings safety paralyzed in a motorcycle accident, wrote that prior to the accident he was mostly pursuing worldly pleasures. Kassulke reflected:

"Fun was all I was living for. . . . and those times were not enough to fill the empty void in my soul. . . . I look at people, and I see them trying so hard to reach for something they cannot get, or can't even define. I see them absorbed in money or success or status, and I say to myself, 'Yeah, Karl, baby. You've gone through that stuff, but now you're whole. You don't need it.'"[86]

The Old Testament book of Ecclesiastes tells a classic story of emptiness from seeking self-gratifying worldly pleasures and significance. King Solomon concluded that all his lifelong accumulations of wealth, women, power, work, possessions, and earthly pleasures led only to vanity -- to an empty life. Solomon writes:

"I undertook great projects: I built houses for myself and planted vineyards. I made gardens and parks and planted all kinds of fruit trees in them. I made reservoirs to water groves of flourishing trees. . . . I owned more herds and flocks than anyone in Jerusalem before me. I amassed silver and gold for myself, and the treasure of kings and provinces. I acquired male and female singers and a harem, as well – the delights of a man's heart. I became greater by far than anyone in Jerusalem before me. In all this my wisdom stayed with me. I denied myself nothing my eyes desired; I refused my heart no pleasure. My heart took delight in all my labor, and this was the reward for all my toil. Yet when I surveyed all that my hands had done and what I had toiled to achieve, everything was meaningless, a chasing after the wind; nothing was gained under the sun" (Ecclesiastes 2:4-6,7b-11).

The Bible says, "For where you have envy and selfish ambition, there you find disorder and every evil practice" (James 3:16). Sadly many people die having lived by the words of *M.T. Self*. People stretch the truth at their funerals, struggling to find real meaning in their life.

If you listen to *M.T.'s* lies about how to find pleasure and significance you will not grow close to God. The life filled with self-pleasure and self-significance has no room for God. You will not have a heart transforming in the direction of Jesus' likeness. And you will not have an impact on others that lasts into eternity. Your life will be wasted, defeated by the enemy.

King Solomon eventually realized that a life focused on his own achievements did not lead to joy; but that satisfaction and true meaning come when we center life on attentiveness to God. He wrote, "Here is the conclusion of the matter: fear God and keep his commandments, for this is the duty of all mankind" (from Ecclesiastes 12:13).

Jumping ahead about 3000 years, quarterback Randall Cunningham discovered the truth in Solomon's words. He admitted that when he came into the NFL his focus was in the wrong place. "I was more about me than anyone else," wrote Cunningham. Through a variety of life experiences and mentoring by others he came to the conclusion,

"Life is not about you. . . . This life is not about building up our own glory. Rather, it's all about pursuing God and realizing our life as it stands in relation to him."[87]

Author and pastor Rick Warren reached the same Biblically-based conclusion as Cunningham. He writes in *The Purpose Driven Life:*

"The purpose of your life is far greater than your own personal fulfillment, your peace of mind or even your happiness. It's far greater than your family, your career, or even your wildest dreams and ambitions. If you want to know why you were placed on this planet, you must begin with God." Warren later continues, "It is only in God that we discover our origin, our identity, our meaning, our purpose, our significance and our destiny. Every other path leads to a dead end. Life is about letting God use you for His purposes, not you using Him for your own purpose."[88]

If our self-gratification is the objective of life, we will never be satisfied. Barry Sanders concluded what many have come to realize, "Only God can ever satisfy the hunger inside of you."[89]

Losing Yourself

Jesus did not come to us to say, "Go and find what brings you pleasure and do it." He didn't say, "God has a wonderful plan that is centered on you - for making your life happy and personally fulfilling." On the contrary, He directs us to take the stadium lights off ourselves and shine them on God and others. Jesus clearly and concisely states your mission: "You must love the Lord with all your heart, all your soul, all your strength, and all your mind" and "love your neighbor as yourself" (see Luke 10:27 and Matthew 22:37-40).

Jesus came to alter the way humanity approaches life - losing our self-centeredness and exchanging that for a God-centered life. And through that exchange, other relationships gradually become right and healthy.

Jesus' life is the supreme example of not looking out for your own interests, but rather for the interests of others. He left heaven to enter into an earthly life of trials, difficulties, homelessness, pain, ridicule, and an excruciating death. His heart was completely unselfish. Jesus thought of others even as he was being crucified. While nailed to the cross, He asked a friend to take care of His mother, promised paradise to a man hanging on the cross next to him, and asked that those crucifying him be forgiven. He cared infinitely more about serving the will of His heavenly Father and His people than He did His own comfort and personal desires.

Jesus died so that we also might shift our inward-focused lives to outward-focused lives centered on Him. The Bible says, "And he died for all, that those who live should no longer live for themselves but for him who died for them and was raised again" (2 Corinthians 5:15).

Jesus said that we need to lose ourselves before we gain. He said, "Whoever wants to be my disciple must deny themselves and take up their cross and follow me" (Mark 8:34; see also Matthew 16:24-26).

Denying yourself… giving up what we want to instead carry the bloody cross… this takes trust. It goes against our whole notion of how to find happiness. It goes against our culture of self-indulgence. It goes against *M.T. Self*'s cry, "It will take away your fun."

Jesus calls you to trust Him… to trust that if you give up putting your self-interests first, and instead sacrificially center on God, He will lead you to a full and meaningful life. This kind of life will also lead to joy. Jesus tells his disciples that His joy would be in them and that their joy would be complete as they remain in His love and live as He taught them to live (see John 15:9-11).

Joy overflowed in the life of Jesus' disciple Peter even though he was going through tribulations. Peter wrote, "Even though you do not see him now, you believe in him and are filled with an inexpressible and glorious joy" (1 Peter 1:8b). Joy exists in the hearts of Jesus' followers even though the daily circumstances are often difficult, painful, and taxing.

Joy is not the fleeting happiness offered by our culture, but a deeply rooted inner sense of pleasure and peace. This kind of real sustaining pleasure comes when we live like Jesus, shifting our attention away from our own happiness and onto loving God and others.

M.T. Self's materialistic and shallow offers will lead to emptiness, jealousy, greed, and dissatisfaction. Jesus lifts us out of the dark pit of a life aimed at finding our next feel-good moment. He brings us into the light of a life joyfully lived for Him and others… a life of true significance.

Real Significance

If you are fortunate enough to one day become old and feeble, and you look back on your life, what will you consider meaningful and significant? You certainly will not be thinking what *M.T. Self* sold you is meaningful or significant. When we try to find significance through our wealth, power, prestige, status, materialistic accumulations and/or knowledge, we will be so self-focused that a relationship with God, a changing heart, and love for others will be greatly thwarted.

True significance starts from our position as a child of God, created magnificently unique and beautiful by the power of the Almighty. You're significant apart from what you do, but rather by Whose you are.

Yet even when we understand our inherent significance as a child of God, most guys still want tangible and specific ways their life can be impactful. We not only want to be on the team, we want to get out and play and make a difference for the team. The Bible says, "For we are God's handiwork created in Christ Jesus *to do good works*, which God prepared in advance for us to do" (Ephesians 2:10 – italics added). God made us "to do good works."

Significance results when our good works show the heart of God in action. God is glorified when our unique personality, desires, talents, and life experiences are taken into the world to help others meet their physical, emotional and spiritual needs. Significance is less about *what* we do and mostly about *who* we do it for and *who* is at the center of it all.

M.T. Self is knocked off his feet when Jesus is at the center of all works of service, all accomplishments, all accolades and all worship. When you follow Jesus, your simplest deeds to your greatest accomplishments are all done for the glory of God. With the right motivation and focus, fulfillment can come from all areas of your life, including work, family, volunteering, recreation, and friendships.

Significance at Work

God wires most men for work – to design, construct, organize, fix and heal. Work brings satisfaction and significance. But if our purpose at work is independent from glorifying God, and mostly revolves around me and my self-image and my rewards, *M.T.* will tackle you hard. If your work regularly pulls you out of balance from fulfilling your other purposes, such as leading your family, serving your community and growing close to God, *M.T.* has nailed you.

Working for the right reasons fulfills several important purposes God has for us. Our salary supports our family and can be donated to help the needy and glorify God. Significance can come from helping a business succeed and thereby provide employment and income for other families. People may also benefit from the services or products produced at your work.

Additionally, work fits into God's plan when you cast a light in the workplace. Work is often a major point of intersection with other's lives. Victory at work comes from modeling excellence, integrity, ethics and compassion to coworkers, and helping them to see the love of Christ in action.

Raven's 13-time Pro Bowler Ray Lewis emphasizes that it's not enough to just be good at your job. "If you don't serve others and genuinely seek to make everyone around you better, your talent won't matter."[90]

When we follow Jesus, our work is not all about our self. It's not about feeding our pride. Instead it is centered on using our talent for serving God and others.

Significance with Family

Your God-given purpose in the home is to love and support your wife and kids, taking initiative to sacrifice your own wants for the needs of the family. The Bible says, "Husbands, love your wives, just as Christ loved the church and gave himself up for her" (Ephesians 5:25). Loving, honoring, and sacrificing for your wife is commanded by God. *M.T.* will have a hard time gaining leverage for his purposes when you lead your family by bringing your wife: love, support, companionship, protection, romance and an abundance of your time and focused attention.

Placing a high priority on your relationship with your wife is also foundational in your role as a father. A strong marriage is a tremendous blessing to your kids. Significance as a Father also involves entering daily into your kids' world. Quarterback Randall Cunningham wrote,

> "The building blocks of our culture start with strong families, and the father is vital to the equation. Children need fathers who are present. They need to be taught by

their fathers, encouraged by their fathers, loved by their fathers." [91]

The Bible directs dads to raise their kids in the training and instruction of the Lord (see Ephesians 6:4) and to place God's commands on their child's heart (see Deuteronomy 6:5-7).

Your legacy into future generations depends on how well you fulfill your role at home – showing love, living out truths in the Bible, and disciplining in love. The whole family is blessed incredibly when the man is not living for himself, but instead follows Jesus and sacrifices to make his relationships with his wife and kids (and grandchildren) central to his life's calling.

Significance in Helping Others

Walter Payton came to recognize that his abilities were given to him for meeting needs of other people rather than his own. Payton writes:

> "Does God care that I could run the ball better than most? Obviously God gave me that ability, but I was always questioning why he gave me that ability. He didn't do it so I could become rich and famous. He didn't do it so I could make the hall of fame or help the Bears win the Super Bowl. He must have done it so I could use my fame and my popularity to rally people and help others." [92]

Payton established a foundation to help inner city schools and to bring Christmas presents to the poor. Payton used his gifts, talents and life experiences to reach out in love to others beyond his work and family.

Your upbringing, talents, good and bad experiences, and personality, are not like anyone else's in the world. So when it comes to loving others, you can do it like no other person. It might be mentoring others, helping a neighbor, visiting the sick and elderly, praying for those in need, volunteering at food shelves, building homes for the poor, going on church mission trips, spreading the Gospel, or bringing encouragement to the downtrodden. The key is letting the love of Christ flow through you and out into the world.

As you volunteer to help others, be aware that *M.T. Self* wants to torture you by having you constantly assess the adequacy of your volunteering efforts. "Have you piled up a high enough mound of good works?" questions *M.T.* Don't fall for this self-focused trap set by *Self.* He's only trying to shift the spotlight back on to you.

M.T. will also try to twist the motivation for your volunteer mission work, making it all about satisfying your own sense of worth. The real purpose of your service is not to feel good about yourself, but to love and bless others, and in the process glorify God.

Troy Vincent, defensive back for the Eagles, sums it up well in *Sports Spectrum Magazine*, stating:

> "What really matters is . . . just blessing people, just building up people and being there for people. At the end of the day, it's all about people. And that's what Jesus was, a healer, a provider, and He touched people, met them where their need was, and that's what we have to do here on earth."[93]

It all comes down to following Jesus and "just blessing people."

Significance in Recreation

Men have innate callings to be outside, to be challenged, to compete, to achieve physical goals, to move the body, rest the body, and use different parts of the mind. Most men desire certain times of recreational activity, such as golfing, fishing, hunting, camping, football, or some other hobby that rejuvenates the heart.

God delights in giving His children enjoyment and letting them do things that make their heart soar. But God did not intend that our recreational passions become the objective of our lives. God did not author the t-shirts stating, "Football is Life" and "Fishing is Life."

Is it bad to spend time on recreation instead of helping others? If you're living for recreational activities, if they become the god of your life, then you will be tackled repeatedly by *M.T. Self.* But recreational activities used in healthy proportion can keep you in better shape to resist the devil and pour yourself into the lives of others. Recreation can fulfill inborn callings, renew body and soul, and bring you delight, good health, adventure and camaraderie.

Recreation alone cannot bring significance, but it is part of an overall plan for a significant and victorious life. In appropriate balance, recreation will help you to love God and love others.

By giving you the Sabbath, God emphasizes the importance of regularly taking time away from work to center on God and family and rejuvenation. He knows the importance of keeping your soul refreshed. He does not want to give Spoilers players any footholds.

Significance in Friendships

Real meaning cannot be achieved without connecting in relationship with God and with people. Jesus had a close bunch of friends into whom He poured His life.

When we follow Jesus, we will intentionally spend time in the company of other men. Friendships are not just about having someone to do stuff with. Recreation with friends is important, but friendships become most significant when they allow men to encourage, affirm, support, and strengthen each other. The Bible says, "as iron sharpens iron, so one person sharpens another" (Proverbs 27:17). We sharpen each other when we stand beside each other, reflect on goals and dreams, confidentially discuss personal challenges, and confront one another when veering off course.

By following Jesus, all areas of our life become more fulfilling and joyful, including friendships. A key to all meaningful areas of life is finding a good balance, and recognizing that the right balance will change during the various seasons of life.

M.T. is Smashed

Jesus came to take the lens off of you and your empty striving for happiness and shift that attention onto something much larger than ourselves – onto loving God and others. He showed that victory comes from surrendering your life to the Lord. This replaces the void of a self-focused empty existence with true significance and a shared victory that's much larger than our self.

Jesus also assures us that when we slip back into moments of self-centeredness, our salvation is still secure – that His death on the cross covers all our sin.

"The reason the Son of God appeared was to destroy the devil's work" (1 John 3:8b). By following Jesus, the work of *M.T. Self* is destroyed. You follow, and your Lead Blocker smashes this notorious linebacker.

 Inspired by your teammates, you see the bigger picture… you see beyond yourself. On 1ˢᵗ and 10, you get the ball and follow right behind your Lead Blocker as He throws a key block on M.T.. You pick up 4 yards. 2ⁿᵈ and 6 from the Spoilers 25.

* * *

Huddle questions for Chapter 11 small group discussion are found free online at www.UltimateScoringDrive.com

Chapter 12

Blasting "Past"

2nd and 6 from your opponents 25. You take the handoff and veer toward the outside, picking up a few yards before being cut down by the outside linebacker Red Past. It's not the first time someone missed their block on Red Past and you get a little angry at one of your teammates. 3rd and 3 from the Spoiler's 22.

Deeply Rooted Anger

Football players have plenty to get mad about. Cheap shots and illegal hits are commonplace. Referees make bad calls. Opposing fans yell slanderous remarks. Sometimes even their own fans turn against them. It's hard not to let some of this bother you. Some players hang on to their anger in such a way that it takes away their focus on the game, decreasing their level of play. Some carry resentment beyond the game and beyond the week, just not letting go.

Injustices on the football field can sting. Yet hurts and injustices in life can hurt a lot more. Every man who has been playing this game for a while has been let-down, left out, neglected, abused, or hurt by someone in the past.

Sometimes pain from the past goes back to your upbringing. Kids' worlds are torn apart when their parents' marriage shatters. Some had a father who was absent or abusive. Many sons received injury from their dad's words… words that penetrated so deep that they caused a lifetime of ache and doubt about who they are as a man.

Red Past comes into the game to say, "You have every right to remain angry at your dad. Don't ever trust him. And don't trust anyone else either." To some men *Past* says, "You had to grow up on your own, so don't think you can rely on anyone now, especially God."

Maybe you had a decent upbringing, but later were betrayed or slighted by a friend, employer, co-worker, spouse, neighbor, or a wayward son or daughter. *Past* whispers to you:

> "You're entitled to remain embittered with people who have hurt you. That person has wronged you in such an egregious way that you need to hang on to that resentment. You should never forgive that person."

Red Past hopes that a deeply rooted anger in your heart will get in the way of all three keys to a victorious life… your relationship with God, your transforming heart, and your positive impact on other people.

A person who hurt you in the past may have been another Christian, or even a church leader. They may have embarrassed you, shamed you, cut you out of something, or much worse.

"No way should you ever forgive them," shouts *Red Past*. "They hurt you. Their God obviously is not worth worshipping. How can you trust a God whose church members behave like that? You better just stay away from God and stay away from His church."

Perhaps it is God Himself who let you down. He didn't come through for you. You prayed. You prayed real hard. And still no answer came. He did not answer you how you wanted and when you wanted. Your mom was not miraculously healed. That accident was not prevented. Your longed-for baby never was conceived. The new job didn't come to you. Your daughter's disease has not been healed.

Past and his Spoilers teammate *Suffering* want you to hold on to your anger at God. "Huh… I told you that you couldn't rely on God. How can you trust Him when he didn't listen to your heart-felt request. And you are such a good person. What good is a relationship with Him?"

Removing a Spoilers Foothold

Most men are tackled by *Red Past* at some point. Some get tackled repeatedly by this Spoilers linebacker, halting all significant progress. He needs to get blocked out or taken out.

Your Playbook asks you to reconcile your anger. The Bible says, "In your anger do not sin: Do not let the sun go down while you are still angry, and do not give the devil a foothold" (Ephesians 4:26-27). We cannot let our anger or resentment fester and become a foothold for Satan. *Red Past* wants our anger to remain a red-hot amber burning in our heart, stealing peace, and stealing love.

In the Old Testament, we see King David, "a man after God's own heart," expressing directly to God the full range of human emotions, including frustration and anger. Bottling up such emotions inside is not the Biblical approach to dealing with bitterness from past hurts.

When we look at Jesus' life, we don't see someone who denied the emotion of anger. In Jesus' case, he was angry when He saw the self-serving Pharisees exploiting religion instead of bringing people closer to God (see Mark 11:15-17). Temporary angers are a part of the human experience. In Jesus' case, the angers were righteous.

In cases of severe past abuse, you may need professional help. Sometimes the legal system is needed to bring justice to those who have wronged you. But whether or not hurtful things in your past need the force of law or the assistance of Christian counselors, anger needs to be uprooted from your heart. Jesus came onto the field to help you with such uprooting.

Jesus shows us how to live through past hurts and injustices without letting it stop your scoring drive. He does this by:

1) Showing you how much you are worth to God, regardless of what others have told you or what your past suggests;

2) Assuring His followers forgiveness for their own transgressions against God and others; and

3) Teaching and modeling how to forgive others and love enemies.

When we follow Jesus, He leads us away from heart decay and right past *Red Past*.

You are Treasured

One key to getting beyond *Past* is to come back to the topic of how much you are loved. People who do not understand God's deep love for them often remain embittered from past slights. God came as Jesus to emphasize through His actions and teaching the unconditional love God has for you.

Jesus' story of the prodigal son crystalizes this point (see Luke 15:11-32). The young man in the story leaves his father and family to live a self-centered, sin-filled lifestyle until he's finally broke and broken. As he sheepishly returns to his father, he finds that his father welcomes him back with open arms and throws a big party celebrating his returned son. God welcomes us at any point when we come back to Him, no matter what happened in the past. Jesus made it clear that when you come to Him, God will be there waiting to give you a big hug, and then celebrate your arrival.

Just as the father in God's prodigal son story restored his son's worth and dignity, God does the same with us. You're not a prisoner of your past. You're not what others have said about you in the past, or a product of how others have treated you. You are a new creation in Christ. "Anyone who belongs to Christ has become a new person. The old life is gone; a new life has begun!" (2 Corinthians 5:17 NLT).

God's Son came to earth to be with us and show us how much we mean to Him; so much that He was willing to die for us. He loves us enough to He forgive our repenting hearts of the dirt and grime in our life. He loves us so much that He not only wants to make a home in our heart for Him to reside, but He wants to make us a home in heaven where we can reside together for all of eternity.

Who you are is a beloved child of God who is treasured by Jesus Christ, the Son of God. God forgives you for the hurts and injustices you yourself have wrought against God and others when you repent and humbly return to Him. This love and forgiveness from God gives you the capacity to release your bitterness and anger toward God and others.

Forgiving Others

The Bible says, "Bear with each other and forgive one another if any of you has a grievance against someone. Forgive as the Lord forgave you" (Colossians 3:13).

NFL wide-receiver Derrick Mason was quoted in a *Sports Spectrum Magazine* article,

> "That's what God has instilled in me - love, just love - no matter whether it's your enemy or your brother. Just love 'em. Somebody might do wrong to you, you still love 'em, no matter what the circumstance is. For somebody to do something wrong, you've just got to love that person."[94]

Loving those who have wronged us is not an easy thing to do; at least not through our own power. But with the love of God and power of the Holy Spirit in our heart, we can "just love 'em."

Jesus does not leave us with any question about what we need to do with those who have wronged us in little or big ways, once or innumerable times. God knows the destruction caused in our own lives and in our relationship with Him when we hang on to anger and don't forgive others. He knows that the malignant tumors of anger stuck in the corners of our heart need to be removed so we are set free and can truly live with a changed and victorious heart.

God comes into our lives to lead us to forgive those who sin against us (see Matthew 6:12). Jesus emphasizes the need to forgive others, stating, "For if you forgive other people when they sin against you, your heavenly Father will also forgive you" (Matthew 6:14). When the disciple Peter asked Jesus if a person should forgive another as much as seven times, Jesus responded, "I tell you, not seven times, but seventy-seven times" (Matthew 18:22).

But Jesus did not just talk about the need to forgive others, He did it. As He was hanging in extreme agony on the cross, He asked God to forgive those who were torturing and killing Him (see Luke 23:34). He also restored Peter and implicitly forgave him after Peter denied knowing Jesus three times during the night Jesus was arrested.

The Bible says,

> "Get rid of all bitterness, rage and anger, brawling and slander, along with every form of malice. Be kind and compassionate to one another, forgiving each other, just as in Christ God forgave you" (Ephesians 4:31-32).

Without Jesus leading the way, our unforgiving heart would continue to be tackled by *Past*. By trusting and obeying Jesus, we are able to live with a forgiving heart that's free from bitterness.

The Power of Forgiveness

Some have said that when you forgive others it helps you more than it helps those who have wronged you. You regain freedom from a soured life. Joy is now able to grow and thrive. You can focus on the game at hand, the here and now job of progressing toward the goal line.

But the benefits of forgiving extend well beyond the person doing the forgiving. Forgiving others who have wronged us, especially if they have wronged us in severe ways, is so countercultural that people take great notice. When you not only forgive others, but genuinely love your offenders, people are moved.

Jesus says, "Love your enemies, do good to those who hate you, bless those who curse you, pray for those who mistreat you" (Luke 6:27-28). Jesus asks us to extend a hand to help an opponent up, who on the previous play hit you after the whistle, spat on you and then ground his cleats into your leg. Such a response goes so far against our nature and reasoning that it's the kind of response that can change an enemy's heart. It is a victorious response from someone following their Lead Blocker.

The world wants to know more about what enables you to have the power to release your entitled anger and show love to the unlovable. It is hard for others to keep hatred in their own hearts when they see you living in forgiveness, gratefulness and hope, despite a hurt-filled past.

Some who take notice are going to want to know how you're able to forgive, how you're able to still smile, how you're able to live in peace and thankfulness. God is glorified when others learn that the source of your power to forgive and to live with hope comes from Jesus Christ.

One More Grudge

What if when you truly search your heart you discover that it isn't only another person who has let you down in the past, but it is God Himself? *Red Past* and his teammate *Ben Suffering* smile devilishly when we hold a grudge against God.

God does not always answer our prayers the way we want. Sometimes He seems downright neglectful and absent when we need Him the most. Within a world of freedom, sin, evil, and the inexplicable, we are apt to have times when we wish our all-powerful God would intervene and stop some specific bad thing from happening. Many people resent God because of past disappointments with the way God appeared to not respond.

The apostle Paul did not get his hoped-for answer when he repeatedly pleaded for a troublesome "thorn in his flesh" to be removed from his life. The thorn remained. Paul wrote, "Three times I pleaded with the Lord to take it away from me. But he said to me, 'My grace is sufficient for you, for my power is made perfect in weakness'" (2 Corinthians 12:8-9a). Even the pleas from someone so faithful as Paul were not answered as Paul would have preferred.

Jesus prayed in the Garden of Gethsemane that God the Father would consider some other way to deal with the sin of the world than through His excruciatingly painful flogging and death on the cross. Yet in that moment of anguish, Jesus also prayed that the Father's will would be done. Jesus' plea did not result in a release from his brutal death.

Jesus and Paul trusted that God the Father was in control and that He had the big-picture view of the universe in mind.

When God has disappointed us in the past, we need to confess our bitterness and pray for God's help to release our anger and restore our trust. These times of honest, heart-felt reflection with God can lead us to a closer relationship with Him and ultimately to getting past *Red Past*. If resentment of God remains and is never reconciled, we are in jeopardy of fumbling the ball away and ultimately losing.

Blasting Past Red Past

Filled with thoughts of a Holy and loving God, Jesus' followers are encouraged to release ugly events from the past and live by the words:

"Whatever is true, whatever is noble, whatever is right, whatever is pure, whatever is lovely, whatever is admirable – if anything is excellent or praiseworthy – think about such things" (Philippians 4:8).

Minds filled with God's goodness and gifts are dominated by thankfulness and contentment. Embitterment and negativity are booted away.

The apostle Paul writes:

"But one thing I do: Forgetting what is behind and straining toward what is ahead, I press on toward the goal to win the prize for which God has called me heavenward in Christ Jesus" (Philippians 3:13b-14).

Paul had every reason to be mad at the world. He was mistreated, kicked out of cities, imprisoned, slandered and severely beaten. But with the love of Christ in his heart, his anger was quickly surrendered to God. He looked toward the goal line, trusting in God's sovereignty and knowing that God's justice would prevail in the end. Paul finished the race victoriously.

Paul knew through Christ how much he was treasured by God. He knew how his past life of persecuting Christians was forgiven by God. He knew how much God wanted him to forgive the many people who treated him cruelly. Through Jesus, Paul had the model of how to love and forgive his enemies. He had the power from God to release all anger.

Everything we need for victory we find in following Jesus, including the ability to forgive our transgressors, love our enemies, and trust in God's will. As we follow Him closely, *Past* is history.

With great blocks on *Max Fear, M.T. Self, Ben Suffering and Red Past*, you are trusting God more and more. You're becoming more and more rooted and established in Jesus. Now only three starting defensive players remain between you and the goal line – *Noah*

U. Perfect, Rusty Passivity and *B.N. Busy*. Don't underestimate the resolve of these three to stop you well short of the victorious life God has planned for you.

3ʳᵈ and 3 from the Spoilers 22. A risky double reverse is called. The ball is handed off to your wide receiver who runs the reverse. You lined up on the opposite side from your receiver so that you could take the handoff from him when he runs your way. Red Past reads the play perfectly and heads toward you. Your Lead Blocker fixes His eyes on Past and hits him solidly. You have lots of room to run but then slip on the grass and are hit by the defensive secondary player Noah U. Perfect. You barely picked up the first down. 1ˢᵗ and 10 from the Spoiler's 19.

* * *

Huddle questions for Chapter 12 small group discussion are found free online at www.UltimateScoringDrive.com

Part IV.
Past the Secondary – Growing

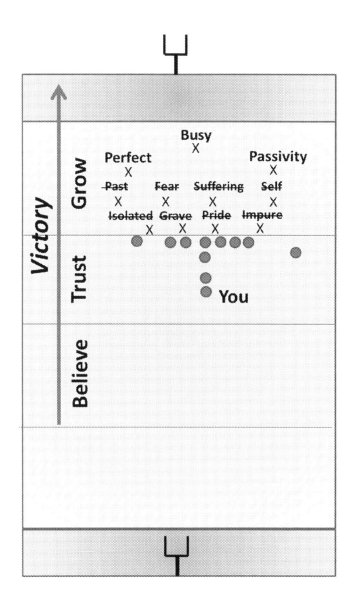

Chapter 13

Destroying "Perfect"

 Returning to the huddle you express your frustration to a teammate. "I should have had a lot more yards on that last play. I can't believe I slipped." "Don't let it bother you," says your teammate, "Nobody is perfect."

Who is Perfect?

"One thing I always worked for was the perfect game," said Walter Payton. "All the time I played the game of football, I was shooting for that perfect game. It never happened. A perfect game is making every fake, catching every pass, doing everything you have to do. People said I had the perfect game against Minnesota because I rushed for 275 yards. But that was a long way from perfect," admitted Payton.[95]

In football, perfection is not achievable by anyone, not even the great Walter Payton, not even for one game. In our faith journey on the field of life, complete perfection is also not achievable, not even for a single day.

The Bible says that God made us in His own image. But that does not mean we are perfect as God is perfect. Churches aren't perfect either. "For all have sinned and fall short of the glory of God" (Romans 3:23).

Some NFL greats are held up high on a pedestal. Ladainian Tomlinson is one such former player. A *Sports Spectrum Magazine* article noted: "Teammates talk of his (Tomlinson's) generosity to strangers and his patience obliging the never-ceasing request for an autograph." Drew Brees remarked about his former teammate and friend, "You can sit here and can't find anything wrong with the guy."[96] But Tomlinson knows he's certainly not perfect. In the same article, He responds to the glowing words about him saying:

> "I don't want to get to the point where people think that I'm some guy who doesn't mess up. I don't want people to get the wrong idea like I'm perfect. . . . Sometimes people get unrealistic views of Christians. Christians are real people. Just because they love God and strive to be perfect like God doesn't mean they don't mess up. Everybody does. The key for me is learning from the mess-ups and trying to get back on the right track." [97]

Kurt Warner, another man admired for his faith walk, admits to his imperfections. He wrote how he's not immune from getting caught up in his own world of self-focus. Warner also importantly noted that as he draws closer to God the self-focused temptations diminish.[98]

Christians certainly have faults. Yet they also know that without their faith they would succumb to more temptations and more easily fall into life patterns of sin.

When Barry Sanders played for the Detroit Lions his model of faith was lifted high by many. He was highly regarded, not only for his amazing running game on the field but for his life off the field. In His book *Barry Sanders – Now You See Him…* Sanders discusses some of his challenges and mistakes, including fathering a baby out of wedlock not long after being involved in making a video for teenagers promoting abstinence until marriage. Sanders admits to making mistakes. Yet he also noted how he would "hate to see how his life would have looked" if he hadn't had his faith, God's grace and a solid upbringing in the Church.[99]

Quarterback Aaron Rodgers also recognizes the challenges a Christian faces in living as Jesus lived. Rodgers admits to "falling on his face," and he's not referring getting sacked. Rodgers rededicated his life to the Lord at age 17, after realizing that what he and his friends were starting to do was not right. He explains, "Ever since then I fall on my face and get back up, get on my knees and confess, and keep on trying to live for Jesus. It's not easy. It's daily dying to yourself and prioritizing your time."[100]

So who is perfect? If we use the word perfect to mean without sin, there is none other than Jesus Christ. The Bible describes a few men as righteously mature and whole hearted, including Noah, Abraham and Job of Old Testament times. But their entire lives were not perfect. A common theme in the Old and New Testament is God working with fallible godly men to do great things. For example, King David was a man after God's own heart, but still had times of failure, such as his moral failures surrounding Bathsheba, which included adultery, deceit and murder (see 2 Samuel 11).

Even one of the most faithful, Christ-centered persons who ever lived, the apostle Paul, admitted his failings. He wrote, "For what I want to do I do not do, but what I hate I do... for I do not do the good I want to do, but the evil I do not want to do – this I keep on doing" (Romans 7:15,19). Paul attributed this to sin living within him. Paul also had a falling out with his faithful friend Barnabas who had been traveling and ministering with Paul for years. They ended up going separate directions for a while. Even the most godly men can have relationship challenges.

Everyone's faith is an imperfect work in progress. We live in a cycle of remembering and forgetting God. We will have times of great spiritual growth, spending time in prayer and serving the Lord. And we will have times when we feel like we are in the desert, when prayer comes hard and God seems distant. Sometimes the well seems empty and we find it difficult to feel God's companionship, comfort, and radiance. Spiritual growth is not a continuous rise throughout each day of our life. We have peaks and valleys.

No one achieves perfection in their thought-life or actions. No one maintains complete purity and complete freedom from pride, fear, doubt and self-interest. No one loves perfectly. No one manages their time perfectly, striking just the right balance between: work and rest, worship and working, time with family and time with strangers in need, being quiet and talking. Your QB calls the plays and gives you guidance, but nobody listens perfectly and executes the plays precisely as they should.

"You Don't Belong in the Game"

The defensive back for the Spoilers, *Noah U. Perfect*, understands that even the most faithful don't approach perfection. He tries hard to convince you that your failings and imperfections disqualify you from playing the game.

"There you go again, messing up... how can you think those thoughts? How could you do that? How could you fail to take that action?" shouts *Perfect*. "True Christians don't think those shameful thoughts or do those things. You're not worthy to be called a Christian... you don't belong in God's family... you just simply are not worthy of God's love... you don't do nearly enough of the things God asks you to do... look at what you're not getting done... you don't give enough. Just get out of the game... it's not for you."

Every time he sees you on the field, *Noah U. Perfect* tries to make you feel unworthy of the Christian faith. Time and time again he talks trash, highlighting another aspect of your imperfect life. *Perfect* hopes to discourage your walk of faith.

"In the lives of maturing Christians, one of the deadliest traps I've seen is the trap of thinking they have to be perfect," writes running back Shaun Alexander. Alexander continues:

> "It's Satan that says you have to be perfect. But God says something different. . . . Perfection is a goal you can't attain in this life. Once it becomes your goal and you

don't reach it, you think you can never reach it, and you give up. That's all Satan wants, so he can defeat you."[101]

Noah U. Perfect is not just an enemy to the maturing Christian, but also to those who have not yet really come to know God. *Perfect* tries to convince them that they are not good enough to approach God. "God is way too holy for the likes of you… so just stay away. Faith is for spiritual superstars. So until you get to that point, just keep your distance from God."

Works in Progress

Another tactic of *Perfect* is to highlight imperfection in the Christian Church and its leadership. "C'mon… how can you trust in a God whose Church behaves like that? Hypocrites… they are just hypocrites."

Perfect hopes you will equate the church with God. He hopes this mistaken notion will lead you to become disillusioned with God when you witness the inevitable conflicts, hurtful remarks, pettiness, cliques, neglect, and hypocrisy coming from a church made of people, of sinners.

The mature believer knows he's a work in progress and so is the Church. Both are under construction by God. The Church is certainly not a perfect representation of God or the teachings and Spirit of Christ. It's made of imperfect people, who have imperfect leaders and staff, who use imperfect constitutions and bylaws, who imperfectly listen to God, and who imperfectly interpret and understand God's Word.

We are not living out what we believe and profess one-hundred percent of the time. Many have said, "The church is not a museum for saints, but a hospital for sinners." A good church consists of fallible people who recognize the need for God's grace and forgiveness. Faithful church-goers want to grow in faith and obedience, and ultimately become more and more like Jesus. But they are not there yet. They are works in progress. We are all works in progress.

Jesus Embraces the Imperfect

Jesus comes into the game to block *Noah U. Perfect.* Jesus spent most of his time with those who were far from perfect -- those who were considered by society as unworthy outcasts. He respectfully and gracefully talked with a woman caught in adultery, a fraudulent tax collector, a heathen woman, a woman from a different religion, a thief, and others. In each case, Jesus worked to make the person whole. Jesus freely gave grace and healing to those who recognized their own inadequacy and their need for help, and who were therefore open to receiving the transforming power He offered.

For those with a hard heart, such as those whose pride or wealth got in the way of recognizing their need for God's grace, Jesus took a different approach. He was less gentle. He sometimes told them shocking things to help them see beyond themselves and their own self-sufficiency, and to help them recognize their real need for God. For example, He said to the rich man who thought he was doing all the right things, "Sell everything you have and give to the poor" (from Luke 18:22). Jesus wanted the man to see that his heart was wrapped up in his possessions.

Jesus chose disciples who were far from perfect. Even after living with Jesus for a couple years, the disciples bickered, repeatedly misunderstood Jesus, were fearful, prideful, and lacked trust and belief. After Jesus' resurrection, the disciples received the Holy Spirit and these imperfect men were used in great ways to spread the word about Jesus and begin the Christian Church.

The Bible's Old and New Testaments tell one story after another of how God used people who were far from perfect to do great things for His Kingdom.

God's Grace

Jesus' mercy and grace to forgive our sins does not mean He's indifferent to us living with indiscretion. After forgiving a woman caught in adultery, Jesus tells her to "go now and leave your life of sin" (John 8:11). Jesus embraces the imperfect, but never lowers the standard.

Jesus challenges us to a high standard of loving others. In reference to loving the hard-to-love, including enemies, Jesus said, "Be perfect, therefore, as your heavenly Father is perfect" (Matthew 5:48). God sets high standards and does not compromise what holiness is all about; but He shows grace when His followers fail to live up to Holy standards.

The point of the Bible is not that we are perfect or that we should be perfect. We will never obtain a perfect score on an entrance exam to heaven. The point is that God is gracious. We are to confess that we are not perfect, that we are sinners with all too often impure motives. Then trust in God's grace, stay in the game, and allow the Holy Spirit and God's Word to transform and lead us in the direction of Christ's likeness. Your repenting heart is perfect in God's eyes because Jesus paid the penalty for the sins of everyone who repents and turns to Him.

Freedom from a High-Performance Mindset

NFL tight end Benjamin Watson discovered that you'll be constantly stressed out if you let your evaluation of your performance, or other's opinions of your performance, affect your mood.[102] "Striving to be good at something is admirable, but obsessing over being perfect is a pitfall," suggests Watson. [103] "Allow yourself to be imperfect."

One of the real challenges for a Christian, is that when you gain a greater awareness of God's standards and holiness you become more aware of how far short you fall. As we grow closer to our Holy God, we are more keenly aware of the Biblical ideals to love others, take care of the poor, read the Bible, pray, keep your thoughts pure, give generously, witness to others, go to church, forgive and forgive, etc.. You read the Bible or hear a sermon and say to yourself, "Good point. I ought to do that more." You feel like you're not making progress because you can see so much more clearly where you "ought" to be. In essence, the closer we get to God the more we see our sin.

We can easily fall into a high-performance mindset, tracking how well we are fulfilling various expectations and responsibilities as a Christian. You inevitably will see a gap between your performance and God's Holiness. You start to think that you need to make yourself more worthy of being loved by God. So you try harder. And you still fall way short. So you try a little harder yet. This way of thinking sucks joy out of your relationship with God.

Too many men are tackled repeatedly by this high performance mindset. It can drive a guy nuts. You're spending time at a church meeting, and *Perfect* says, "Why are you not out there really helping the needy?" So you go out and feed the hungry, and *Perfect* says, "You should be at home with your own family – they are the ones who really need you tonight." So you start spending more time with your wife and kids. Then *Perfect* says, "You know you should be working harder at your business to be able to provide better for your family." On and on it goes.

There is no such thing as a perfect balance. There is no such thing as doing enough. Jesus came so that we could have peace, not frustration. The Bible says when you put your trust with Jesus, you're completely His and you're loved unconditionally, regardless of the chasm between God's holiness and your far-from-perfect life. You made the team. You are declared forgiven by His grace. Your relationship to God is not contingent on your performance. No matter how short you fall, God does not give up on you.

God is not so much interested in a flawless heart as He is in an authentic heart. He's not so much interested in an unblemished mind as He is in a regular renewing of your mind. He's not so much interested in a spotless record as in having you trust the One who can wipe the slate clean. All that is perfect is saved for heaven.

The Bible says that "the law," the list of do's and don'ts, was put in place to help guard us from sin until the day Christ came (see Galatians 3:24). Because Jesus came, we are released from needing the law as our guardian. We are free from the burden of a high performance mindset.

Playing with Instinct

The Bible tells us how to transform our heart and renew our mind. It is not by following a list of what not to do. The key is to surrender your heart to Jesus and allow God's Holy Spirit to take control of your life each and every day. Focus on Jesus; allow Him to change you from the inside out. Then be led by God, His Son, His Holy Spirit and His Word.

In football, we see how certain players play with great instinct, almost a sixth sense. Some have developed a keen ability to know exactly where other players are, knowing when to cut, when to duck, when to pause, when to throw. A wide receiver uses complete instinct to jump for the ball along the sidelines at just the right time, make the catch with one arm, and come down with feet in-bounds. His instinct comes from talent given to him by God, and then advancing his instinctive play through considerable practice and experience.

By following Jesus down the field we can also gain a kind of sixth sense - an instinctual alignment with the heart of God. You increasingly become in-tune and receptive to the Holy Spirit leading your thoughts, decisions and actions. When you have been given the gift of God's grace, you don't need to hold a perfectionist mindset, but rather a Spirit-led heart. A heart growing from abundant time spent with God and His Word will land with feet in bounds most of the time. You won't be playing perfectly. But you'll live in the freedom of a relationship with Jesus where the power and strength to align with God's will comes from the Holy Spirit. You'll humbly live under the control of God's Spirit.

It's important to look daily to God and the Bible for areas of sin needing confession and reconciliation. But you can discard that self-evaluation scorecard. Follow Jesus rather than a self-rating based on a checklist of do's and don'ts.

Noah U. Perfect is Destroyed

A good father loves his kids through tantrums, rebellious behavior, disobedience, failures, and character flaws. All the more so, our grace-filled Heavenly Father loves us through our imperfections and all stages of our spiritual development.

"The truth that makes me rejoice is that I don't have to be perfect; God loves me just the way I am," wrote Karl Kassulke.[104] Jesus came to show you how much He embraces His flawed followers. He came to bring freedom from a performance-based mindset, replacing that simply with a life of following Him and giving yourself to Him, shortcomings and all. As you surrender to God and follow your Lead Blocker, He destroys the work of *Noah U. Perfect.* Your faith continues to grow and you resume your drive down the field.

Everything we need for victory we find in following Jesus Christ, including freedom from being consumed by an evaluation of how close we are to perfection.

 1ˢᵗ and 10 from your opponent's 19. You roll toward the sidelines to receive a perfectly thrown pass. You extend your arms to catch the ball, but then bobble it. Noah U. Perfect

is about ready to hit your ball-juggling arms, when your Lead Blocker comes out of nowhere to level Perfect. You make the catch right before stepping out of bounds. 2nd and 5 from the Spoilers 14-yard line.

* * *

Huddle questions for Chapter 13 small group discussion are found free online at www.UltimateScoringDrive.com

Chapter 14

Pummeling "Passivity"

2nd and 5 from your opponent's 14-yard line. Satisfied with being in field goal position and the likelihood of scoring some points, you start to become complacent, losing your zeal for finishing the drive strong. On the next play, a 10 yard pass to the outside, you do not approach the play with your normal determination. The safety Rusty Passivity easily breaks up the play. 3rd and 5 from the 14.

Lukewarm

The defensive cornerback *"Rusty Passivity,"* who more often goes by *"Passive,"* specializes in the prevent defense. He will allow shorter yardage gains. He's ok with field goals, but he'll do anything to prevent you from reaching the end zone. *Passive* is most happy when you go through the motions of the game and stop well short of an all-in victorious life. He succeeds when you're satisfied with "good enough," rather than giving your heart and soul to the game. His whole aim is to have you slide into a passive faith, where even though you're a Christian, you're no longer a real threat to him or his team.

After tackling you, *Rusty Passivity* whispers in your ear: "You're doing good enough. You're a good person – man, especially compared to that guy over there. You attend church fairly often; you help someone now and then; and you drink and swear a lot less than many people you know," says *Passive*. "It's not like you don't give any of your money away. You pray when there is something you need from God and when someone else is facing an emergency. You've even read the Bible at different points in your life – you're good!"

You listen to *Passive*. You stay shallow and well within your comfort zone, unwilling to confront some things in your life needing attention. You're satisfied with a somewhat vague sense of who God is, without a real desire to find out more. You got the basics down and you're a "good person." So you continue to go through the motions of living out your faith.

"Keep your faith convenient, comfortable and handy, fitting right in with your own plans," says *Passive*. He convinces you to set up your life so that everything will be fine even if God doesn't come through for you.

Jesus used the word "lukewarm" to describe the kind of faith promoted by *Passive*. He called a church "lukewarm" when the people were not openly rejecting God, but were not filled with the kind of spiritual zeal that God desires (see Revelation 3:15-16).

Kurt Warner writes in his book *First Things First* about his lack-luster faith-life before he fully committed his life to God. Warner grew up in the Church and attended Mass off and on into adulthood. Warner reflects:

> "I wasn't reading my Bible, going to Bible studies, or anything like that. My wife Brenda would tell you that I was a good person and I lived my life right. I wasn't into the things that other college guys my age were doing, so I thought I was pretty good."[105]

Mike Singletary similarly admitted that earlier in his life he was a "religious" man with a lukewarm kind of faith. He said that he used the parts of Bible he was comfortable with and "explained away" the other parts. After his heart was transformed, Singletary said he'd now do whatever it takes to "sell out for God."[106]

Far too many Christians never really break out of this pattern of being a "pretty good" religious man. They play the entire game half-heartedly.

Others become fully alive in their faith for a period of time, but then they let it slide -- they rust out. They make some good progress down the field following Jesus, but then start to distance themselves from their Lead Blocker.

The fortunate ones will recognize what is happening before sliding too far. This discovery is described by Steve Farrar in his book *Finishing Strong*:

> "It's silent and subtle as a slow moving shadow. One minute you're sitting in the sun, reading your newspaper, and enjoying the warmth and radiance. Then suddenly you feel cool, and you look up and realize you've been sitting in the shade for some time. The sun and warmth have long since passed by. You're not seeking Jesus Christ the way you once did. You're not hungrily diving into the Word the way you once did. You're not enjoying the company of other believers the way you once did. You're not delighting in quiet walks and talks with God the way you once did. You're in the shadow, a long way from the Son, and you don't even know how you got there or how your heart became so cold."[107]

So many people go to their graves having fallen well-short of finding true joy through their Christian faith. It's not that they are a "bad" person as the culture defines "bad." They may have performed the spiritual disciplines reasonably well – prayer, church attendance, tithing, Bible reading, etc.. But they did not translate this into daily living centered on God. Some reach their funerals having only given God their leftovers.

Before being convicted by the Holy Spirit, NFL wide receiver James Thrash had a lukewarm faith. Thrash recounted for a *Sports Spectrum Magazine* article,

"It was like I could hear God's voice saying to me that it was time to change, that I've been living a lie . . . He told me I was living like a Christian when I was around Christians, but I was living for the world when I was around worldly people. It was like I was a chameleon, blending in with whomever I was around."[108]

How about you? Are you more concerned about your audience of One or your audience of the world? Has Christ transformed your life to the point you would sell out everything for God? Or are you satisfied with a field goal?

Rusty Passivity loves a static, lukewarm devotion to God. He knows such a life will fall well short of the victorious life God plans for you.

All-In

A passive football player who just goes through the motions won't last. He needs to be all-in, fully committed, alert and intentional, or he will be squashed by the opposition. You can't play half-hearted football and expect to win; and you can't play that way in life and expect a victorious outcome.

Jesus came to let us know that in no uncertain terms does victory come from a passive faith of going through the motions, fitting God into your life in some small way. God gives us a very different vision. Jesus didn't come so much to tweak lives, but to transform lives.

Christianity does not mean compartmentalizing faith into one corner of life, separate from the other corners. It does not mean shelving your faith, only to pull it off the shelf when it might be useful to you. In its most victorious sense, Christianity means surrendering to God completely and having your entire being transformed by the power of the Holy Spirit.

Vince Lombardi said that football players have to commit their entire body to the sport, from the bottom of their feet right up to the top of their head. He said that most importantly men need to play with their heart.[109] Lombardi knew that good football players commit more than one part of their body to the game; they commit heart, head and everything.

Cowboys star Emmitt Smith was a fully committed running back who played with tremendous heart, always giving his best. Smith gives God all the glory for everything accomplished on and off the field. He's a man who expresses a desire to remain all-in for the Lord. He wrote in his book *Game On*:

> "Everything I am and every fiber of my being belongs to him. He has been my rock and my Savior, and whatever I have accomplished is due to his presence in my life."[110]

Jesus does not call us to place God at the top of a list, but rather at the center of everything... family, work, friendships, recreation, finances, sleeping, eating, and doing the daily dozen.

Jesus said, "Those of you who do not give up everything you have cannot be my disciples" (Luke 14:33). Jesus calls us to a genuine devotion as we follow Him - to put whole-hearted faith in Him first and foremost. When you follow Jesus the way He asks, you won't live at the line of mediocrity, doing only the minimum and living as close to sin as possible. You won't just *hear* the Word of God, but you will take risks and action to *apply* the Word in obedience. Jesus said, "If you love me, keep my commands" (John 14:15).

People notice a difference when you're all-in, fully-committed to following Jesus. All-Pro center Jeff Saturday's life speaks loudly to others. "Jeff is a real Christian," observed Colts wide receiver coach Clyde Christensen. He stated about Saturday:

> "He's an outdoorsman, a great father, a fun guy, and he has a deep love for the Lord. There is a realness to his Christianity. With some Christians, their Christianity

repulses you. You say, 'If that's what a Christian looks like, then I think I'll pass.' But Jeff Saturday's relationship with the Lord is alive, active, attractive. It's really neat and refreshing." [111]

The last thing *Rusty Passivity* wants to see is men who are fully committed to Jesus Christ. He will work especially hard to steer you toward a sideline role in some key areas of life, such as leading your family, protecting your sexual purity, and loving others.

Leading Your Family

What sort of priority and intentionality do you place on your marriage and leading your family in areas such as faith?

Our male brains were made different than our wives. The differences are present in the womb and are recognizable at every stage of human development. These differences were designed by God, and they lend themselves to different areas of leadership within the home. God's plan is beautiful – mother and father within the same home, each bringing their different strengths into family relationships, rearing the kids and attending to the home-front.

Satan's player *Passive* has made great strides in messing up a man's role and confusing his purpose within the home. The family, the fundamental God-ordained institution where faith is nurtured, has been under assault by *Passive* for years, especially the man's role within that institution. The result is that far too many husbands and fathers have either rusted out in their recliner or have hid somewhere away from the heart of family interaction.

Passive knows that the entire family suffers when men fall short of fulfilling their purpose in the home. Stu Weber, author of *Four Pillars of a Man's Heart*, states it this way, "When men are not men, civilization falls. When men let their masculinity drift with the winds of culture, everyone loses. When a culture is castrated, it dies."[112] Passivity is not an option for a man of God in his own home.

When men are leading their family in Biblical ways… loving, encouraging, sacrificing, providing, and building peace and security, then everyone flourishes. When you as a man actively and courageously lead with tender sensitivity and unswerving loyalty, often putting your wife's and kids' interests above your own, you will be following God's plan and *Passive* will be dealt a major blow. When you take action to lead your family on the major things, love your wife, and bestow dignity and worth to everyone, you're moving the ball downfield.

Satan's player *Rusty Passivity* works particularly hard at eroding marriages. He knows that a strong marriage centered on Jesus is a victory cornerstone that glorifies God presently and into future generations. *Rusty* loves to see a man take a passive approach to marriage… avoiding the hard work of maintaining a solid marriage. He whispers, "Your marriage doesn't need your attention. Your wife is fine without your devoted time and energies." A passive husband takes his marriage for granted. He does not have daily conversation with his wife, does not plan dates regularly, and does not express appreciation and adoration. Instead of making his marriage the highest priority in his life next to his relationship with the Lord, he passively lets it slide.

Jesus emphasizes the importance of a divorce-proof marriage. He quotes the Old Testament verse, "The two shall become one flesh" (see Matthew 19:5 and Genesis 2:24). Then Jesus stresses a life-long dedication to our wife (see Matthew Chapters 19 and 5).

Protecting Sexual Purity

How carefully do you guard your sexual purity? Do you let your mind passively go where it wants to go? Or do you battle hard for a pure heart?

Passive, in alliance with *Impure,* will work like everything to twist the God-given gift of human sexuality and throw you completely off God's game plan for victory. *Passive* says, "Why resist your natural desires? Don't even try to fight it. Don't challenge your thoughts and feelings. Give in. Check out that girl on TV... and the one walking down the street. Let your mind run unchecked... pornography won't hurt... dwell on your fantasy... flirt with that woman." Major league fumble!

Sexual purity is in the middle of the battlefield with Satan. The Spoilers know that if they can control that part of a man, they will take control of the game. You simply cannot devote your life to God and others when sexual impurity holds a reign on you.

Your Playbook shows you what to strive for. Jesus renounces lust of the eyes in Matthew 5:27-30. The apostle Paul writes, "But among you there must not be even a hint of sexual immorality, or of any kind of impurity, or of greed, because these are improper for God's holy people" (Ephesians 5:3).

The battle for purity is not won by passively letting down your guard. Action is needed to armor yourself and not let that armor rust out. Fill your heart and mind with Jesus. Immediately take impure thoughts and make those thoughts captive and obedient to Christ (see 2 Corinthians 10:5). Clench your Lead Blocker's jersey and run together hard and fast away from impure temptations.

Loving Others

NFL linebacker London Fletcher, who started a program to help underprivileged kids in several cities, said his favorite Bible Verse is James 1:22, which says, "Do not merely listen to the word, and so deceive yourselves. Do what it says."[113] The Bible repeatedly asks that you love others.

When it comes to loving others are you generally passive, only taking action when you feel like it? Or do you intentionally show love to those who are naturally hard to love?

The passive man is stirred by stories about people who personally sacrifice to help others, but he does not get off the bench to take similar action. Jesus does not say to go about life minding your own business, asking for nothing and giving nothing. As soon as you begin a relationship with God, He begins to move you in the direction of translating love into action.

Responding to the slightest inward prompting to show concern and compassion to another, God's love will often flow with ease right out of a heart surrendered to Christ. Yet at other times, taking action to love requires a sheer act of the will. An intentional man does not always let his feelings and emotions drive his actions. Emmitt Smith notes, "You aren't all in if you do your best only when you feel like it, when it's convenient, or when there are no challenges."[114] Intentional men love others as called by God, even when they don't "feel" like doing so.

Rusty Passivity doesn't get so upset when you love other people. "But save your loving actions only for those who will love you in return," says *Passive*. "Certainly don't show loving kindness to those who might not appreciate it, those whom you will never see again, or those who have never shown you kindness. Only show love when it's convenient for you and won't demand too much time and effort."

Jesus calls for a radically different approach, stating:

> "If you love those who love you, what reward will you get? Are not even the tax collectors doing that? And if you greet only your own people, what are you doing more than others? Do not even pagans do that?" (Matthew 5:46-47).

Jesus felt so strongly about taking action to love others, He said that whatever you do to help the hungry, poor, imprisoned, sick, thirsty or lonely, is essentially the same as taking that action to help Him (see Matthew 25:37-40). Jesus also tells the story of the good Samaritan to further emphasize the importance of showing love to others in need (see Luke 10:30-37). In Jesus' story, two men traveling through the countryside walked right by an injured man without helping him. They were fearful and passive. Then a Samaritan man sees the injured man and takes personal risk and sacrifices time and money to help the stranger in need.

Jesus asks His followers to go to extremes to care for people whose lives intersect their own. It does not matter how repulsive or wrong the people are, they're to be loved all the same. Followers of Jesus are called to act compassionately and inconveniently to bring warmth and love to the unloved. Jesus' disciple John wrote, "Let us not love with words or speech but with actions and in truth" (1 John 3:18).

When we love others, we will take action to be the hands and feet of God. We will humbly and respectfully share time, resources and faith with those in need. This will open doors to tell what God has done in our life. One of the most loving things we can do is to share our faith with others... to be a part of helping people discover the wonder, joy and peace that comes from a life lived victoriously in Christ.

Another Cornerback is Pounded Down

Rusty Passivity has been successful in our culture, squelching a man's intentionality to lead his family, protect purity, and compassionately help others. Your Lead Blocker stepped onto the field with you to lead you into taking action in these key areas, in addition to others.

By following Jesus, you won't rust out on the bench. Jesus' life, words and transforming power change a passive life into a passionate life. He calls us away from a complacent religious life and into a fully alive faith. Jesus' love for you transforms half-hearted play into zeal. You begin showing love to those who are hard to love. You're obedient to God even when you don't feel like it. You live an intentional life of growing closer to God and spreading His unconditional love to others, beginning right in your own home.

Following Jesus does NOT mean that you will be working your way into heaven. When you follow Jesus, you are in the family. You're on the team already. You're not going to get cut from the team. Your entrance into heaven and worthiness are not based on the number of stars on your helmet. The Christian faith is not about proving your worthiness before God. It's about letting God's love and the work of God's Holy Spirit guide you into action, bringing you strength, power and wisdom to take leadership in key areas of life.

When you follow Jesus, your Lead Blocker pummels *Rusty Passivity*, destroying yet another opposing player in the way of victory.

Everything we need for victory we find in following Jesus, including the need to overcome our tendency to coast through life. You will finish the drive passionately. You will finish strong.

3rd and 5 from the opposition's 14. In the huddle, your Lead Blocker encourages you to give all your heart and soul to the rest of the game. Re-energized through Him, you take the handoff and hit the hole with great speed. You stay right on the heels of your Lead Blocker as He bowls over one player after another, including Passive. You gain 7. 1st and goal from the 7.

* * *

Huddle questions for Chapter 14 small group discussion are found free online at www.UltimateScoringDrive.com

Chapter 15

Silencing "Busy"

1st and goal from the 7. On the way back to the huddle you help pull up a couple of your teammates. You then stop to consult with a referee about what you thought was a late hit on the previous play. Getting nowhere with that conversation you look to your bench and can see that your teammates support your plea. You try to read the lips of a friend calling out something from the sidelines. You ask him to repeat it but you still can't hear what he's saying. Arriving late in the huddle, you're trying to fix your chinstrap. Through the various distractions, you mishear the called play. Your QB hands you the ball and you take it in the wrong direction and get hit immediately by B.N. Busy. Loss of 1. 2nd and goal from the Spoiler's 8-yard line.

A No-Huddle Offense

Our world right now, more than at any other time in history, is a world of distractions. We are addicted to pre-occupations... most of which take us away from thoughts of God and contemplation of His Word. Living in the age of technology and opportunity, we are enticed inside our home with TV channels galore, movies at our fingertips, an abundance of entertainment and information on the internet, and cell phones blitzing us with texts, notices and calls.

Outside our home, we have ample opportunities to attend sporting events, concerts, and church events. We can hunt, fish, golf, and play softball. We have lots to read – mail, newspapers, magazines, internet blogs, and books. We have careers... we have hobbies and interests... we have home improvement projects... car maintenance projects... and we have our kids' or grandkid's sports and activities. Sometimes we complain about the busyness.

But more often we don't mind… staying busy makes us feel important, entertained, and distracted from some hard things going on around us.

Many men are constantly being tackled by the All-Pro safety *B.N. Busy*. Our busyness is a barrier between us and God, even when we mean well and do good things. If *B.N. Busy* can get us running in circles like a dog chasing its tail, he knows we'll stall-out in our drive down the field of life. He knows our relationship with God will suffer. God won't be first. He won't be heard. And our soul will be injured.

If you're like many men, you buy into *Busy's* devious strategy. You stay with the no-huddle offense, not taking time to regroup with your QB, Lead Blocker or other teammates between plays. No timeouts to hear words from your Team Leader. No time to look at your Playbook. No time to examine your life and your priorities. You just run one play after another. You are even too busy to realize that you're filling all your time with busyness.

B.N. Busy wants you off balance, making sure that other activities substitute for your relationships with God, wife, family and friends. *Busy* would like to lead you away from a healthy balance between being and doing, between intimacy and action, between reflection and compassion. *Busy* wants your faith static or declining, rather than dynamic and growing.

"You have come so far in your faith," says *B.N. Busy*. "You're way down the field… you have grown so much… and are so strong… you can take on all this stuff and do all these things. You're well beyond the need to spend regular time with God praying and studying His Word. Just keep doing stuff. You're not going to accomplish much if you slow down to spend time with God." *B.N. Busy* especially loves it when you spend time succeeding at things that don't really matter in the big scheme of life.

B.N. Busy and his Spoilers teammates will eventually hit you if you get too busy and distracted to huddle with God. They nail you if you don't huddle long enough with God to find clarity of vision and purpose, and to prepare yourself for attacks from the enemy. You'll end up on your butt if you remain too busy to delight in your friendship with God, draw strength from Him, and just share lives with Him.

How about you? Have you gotten yourself busy and distracted, believing it's ok to let your Bible collect dust. Have you put your relationship with God on autopilot? If you have, you may have concluded that faith isn't working like you think it should.

Many men neglect their time with God and at some point conclude that Christianity does not work for them. They don't feel peace, joy, hope, and love enveloping them. Life's challenges are mounting and they don't feel victorious.

Shaun Alexander wisely concluded,

> "You never become so mature that you don't have to constantly watch, fight, and pray. . . . You can be trapped by the lie that you don't need to keep getting stronger in your faith, that you no longer need to prepare for the next battle with the enemy."[115]

Eyes on Jesus

As you try to figure out how to blast through this *Busy* barrier between you and the end zone, God asks you to look at Jesus and follow Him. When you look at the life of Jesus, you see that He walked from town to town, constantly teaching his disciples and others (see Mark 1:32-34 and Mark 3:20-21 Mark 4:35-38). When He arrived in town, swarms of people would surround him, call out to him, touch him, and desperately want Him to heal them or speak to them. The needs and demands were great. Jesus worked hard to compassionately address the needs.

Jesus also made sure to withdraw from activity and have times of solitude with God the Father. He made it a priority to regularly listen to and talk to His Father in heaven. The Gospel of Mark notes, "Very early in the morning, while it was still dark, Jesus got up, left the house and went off to a solitary place, where he prayed" (Mark 1:35). The Gospel of Luke emphasizes that Jesus did not just pray occasionally. It says, "Jesus *often* withdrew to lonely places and prayed" (Luke 5:16 italics added).

Before He began his ministry, Jesus went into the wilderness for an extended period of fasting and praying. Jesus went into solitude when He heard that John the Baptist died; when he was going to choose his disciples; after he healed a leper; and in the Garden of Gethsemane before He was arrested.

But Jesus did not just pray during quiet solitary times; He interjected prayer into the ongoing affairs of the day. Jesus prayed for the protection of others (John 17:11), the needs of others (Matt 19:13; Luke 22:32; John 17:15, 24); and for the unity of believers as God resides in them (John 17:20-21). He praised God (Luke 10:21). He thanked God (Mark 14:22). He sought the Father's will (Matthew 26:39). Jesus gave us a model of both quiet-time prayer and of praying while in action.

Sharing Lives

By following Jesus' example, you will have regular solitary times spent with the Lord, and you will share your ongoing life activities with God. Whatever you're doing – walking, laughing, working or relaxing - you can connect with God by praising Him, thanking Him, talking with Him, enjoying Him and asking Him. You don't need a sacred place to encounter God. You don't need to communicate through theologians, pastors and priests. God is present with you everywhere.

"It's constant prayer – constant, constant, constant prayer," stated Pro Bowl strong safety for the Steelers Troy Polamalu. Polamalu continues, "I think that's a struggle of every Christian, to be able to get to that point where they're in constant prayer with God – so that in everything they do, in thought, in speech, in work, is praising God and worshipping God."[116]

Constant prayer means a heart continuously connected to the Holy Spirit living within you. Aware of God's presence in everything, you turn to Him throughout the day, holding short huddles at meal times, breaks, in the shower, while driving, while exercising, and even while falling asleep and awakening. A.W. Tozer calls this the "habit of inwardly gazing upon God."[117]

Jesus desires that we share our lives with Him. He knows such closeness with Him will lead you to victory.

Huddling with God

In the Gospel of Luke, Jesus drives home the importance of taking time out from serving God to just be with Him. From Luke, we read:

> "As Jesus and his disciples were on their way, he came to a village where a woman named Martha opened her home to him. She had a sister called Mary, who sat at the Lord's feet listening to what he said. But Martha was distracted by all the preparations that had to be made. She came to him and asked, 'Lord, don't you care that my sister has left me to do the work by myself? Tell her to help me!' 'Martha, Martha,' the Lord answered, 'you are worried and upset about many things, but few things are needed—or indeed only one. Mary has chosen what is better, and it will not be taken away from her'" (Luke 10:38-42).

God tells us through His words to Martha that there is great value in just sitting at the feet of the Lord. The natural inclination for many guys is to "do," not just "be." This notion of *being with* God instead of *doing for* God goes against our natural drive. *B.N.*

Busy keeps tackling us. Our fleshly desire is to continuously accomplish, fix, solve, build, or otherwise place our mind into a sport, action movie, or news from around the world.

Like Martha, do you get busy doing so much good stuff that you lose sight of the need to huddle with Jesus, enjoy his words and grace, and be lost in the beauty of his presence? Do you take time to just praise, adore, and thank the God of the universe and His Son? Do you share what is on your heart, including your confessions of sin and failures?

The Bible says, "Be still and know that I am God" (Psalm 46:10a). Your scoring drive will fall short if you get into a no-huddle mindset and fail to set aside your productivity each day to just be with God and delight in Him.

Packers star Reggie White said that prayer can be used for a lot of things, "but most important, prayer should be used to build a relationship with God and to come to know His voice."[118] Faith takes time. Relationships take time. Love takes time. We can't expect to have it instantaneously. In an age of instant everything, we need to take the time, have the patience, enter the stillness, and cultivate a time to just be with God and hear His voice.

Psalm 91:1-2 says, "Whoever dwells in the shelter of the Most High will rest in the shadow of the Almighty. I will say of the Lord, 'He is my refuge and my fortress, my God, in whom I trust.'" How often do we take the time to just "rest in the shadow of the Almighty?"

When you huddle with God and rest in His shadow, you will be: 1) prepared for the daily and weekly battles; 2) getting recharged and refreshed; and 3) better understanding God's will and plans for your life.

Being Prepared

A football player cannot just constantly play the game – skipping huddles, skipping team meetings, skipping practice, skipping game films – only playing the game. It doesn't work for football, and it also does not work for faith. With football and faith, we can't stay so busy that we don't take time to learn, strengthen and prepare.

Victorious football players prepare – they work hard during the off-season and prepare daily during the season. Hall of fame wide receiver Jerry Rice used his off-season for grueling workouts so that he was physically stronger for the season. He writes:

> "Three times a week we would run up a two and a half mile hill, running against the clock. The last eight hundred yards was a steep incline . . . if you couldn't endure the pain, if you couldn't see yourself at the top level in the fourth quarter, the hill wasn't for you. I was in such good condition from running the hill that during the season, there was little difference in my play from the start of the game until the final whistle. . . . The way in which you prepare for a challenge is usually related to your success in that same challenge."[119]

Walter Payton emphasized the importance of mental preparation, writing:

> "The game of football is about 85 percent mental. Sure you have to be able to physically play, but you have to deal with the losses and get yourself mentally ready to go back for another week."[120]

In football, you want to be so prepared that you can react instinctively on the field. You often don't have time to slowly and carefully consider options and decisions when your opposition is crashing down on you. Everything happens fast. You need to rely on the agility and instincts developed during years of practice and play, and from the more immediate preparation during the previous week.

Bible reading, worship and prayer are three key spiritual disciplines that will keep you prepared. Worship service sets you up for the week. Bible reading and prayer sets you up for the day. The Bible is your playbook and game films combined. By studying the Bible, you will have direction for your life and learn what worked and did not work in past games against similarly tough opponents.

Tony Dungy noted in his book *Quiet Strength* what many have discovered - that his daily Bible reading so often fits precisely with what's happening in his life at the time of reading. "Walking closely with the Lord, trusting Jesus, and looking to the Bible for guidance," are three keys to Dungy's daily walk.[121]

Regular time with God and His Word prepares you for the inevitable bumps and turns in life. During the big hits, you won't get knocked silly. If you are prepared through your quiet times with God, the inevitable uncertainty and confusion you will face as a Christian will drive you closer to God rather than push you away.

Jesus says that those who hear God's Word and retain it are like seed falling on good soil where roots can grow deep and produce a large crop (see Luke 8:4-15). He also says that those who come to Him, listen to His words, and put them into practice are like a house built with a solid foundation on rock (see Luke 6:47-49). Satan and life's distractions and troubles are not going to uproot the deep rooted plants or knock down the house constructed on a firm foundation.

With time in God's Word, prayer and worship, you will be more alert, confident, courageous and persevering amidst Satan's blitzes. You will not get burned out and run down to the point of being defenseless. Mental and spiritual preparedness gives you ears to hear God's voice, eyes to see the vision of where you're heading, and instinct to react well on the field.

Recharging Your Spiritual Batteries

Love and a frenzied pace are not compatible. Love takes time. And time is one thing overextended people don't have. Resting with Jesus will renew your capacity to love.

When the disciples returned from a busy time of ministry, Jesus told them, "Come with me by yourselves to a quiet place and get some rest" (Mark 6:31b). Jesus said, "Come to me, all you who are weary and burdened, and I will give you rest. Take my yoke upon you and learn from me, for I am gentle and humble in heart, and you will find rest for your souls" (Matthew 11:28-29).

Jesus comes to you and says, "Rest with me and lay your burdens on me." He says, "Come to the fountains with me and drink of the living water." Jesus wants you to take care of the poor, to stand up for the oppressed, to use your talents to serve others in meaningful ways, to provide for your family, and all of that. But He also insists you rest with Him. If you're burned out, beat up, and run down, what good are you to anyone? In the scoring drive of life, the no-huddle offense cannot be run continuously.

Rejuvenation and renewal through time with God is not meant to be a once-a-year Christmas vacation. "The Christian needs to recharge his spiritual batteries every day," notes Patrick Morley. "The Christian pilgrimage is a moment-by-moment, daily journey. It requires daily effort, without which we will stray."[122]

God asks that we huddle with Him before almost every play. He asks, with our best interests in mind, that we take a long time-out every week. It has been said that we do not keep the Sabbath, but the Sabbath keeps us. Men were not built for a no-huddle way of life. We are hardwired for needing regular times of rest and renewal.

Listening for God's Will

In football, there is no replacement for years of playing experience. In faith, your years of daily and weekly time with God cultivate a greater awareness of God's presence.

B.N. Busy would prefer that you never spend enough time with God to develop a keen sense of His presence and His will. *B.N. Busy* says, "Just pour out your catalog of requests to God, and then check that task off your list for the week." God, on the other hand, asks you to slow down -- to look up and meet His eyes looking down at you, and then hear and sense the things of the Spirit.

Jesus said, "I have come down from heaven not to do my own will but the will of Him who sent me" (John 6:38). Jesus taught us to pray that God's will would be done (Matthew 6:5-15), and He prayed in His own life that God the Father's will would be done. Our huddles and timeouts with God are not supposed to be a monologue of wishes and desires. Reggie White noted, "Prayer sometimes consists of sitting down and just being quiet and listening."[123]

God often speaks through quiet whispers, which the Bible calls the "still small voice" of God. We often miss it. God does not force His way into our lives. He offers Himself to us. Whether we recognize and welcome His approach is up to us. We need a slow enough pace to hear the whispers, to feel the nudges, and then respond.

Too often we feel like we are setting up at the line of scrimmage in a stadium with a roaring crowd. There is too much noise in our life to hear our Quarterback's directions. We may not be sure if we are hearing the voice of our Quarterback or the voice of the enemy.

Regular time reading your Bible will allow you to discern God's will from the voice of the enemy. God's written Word is where He instills basic convictions, attitudes, principles, and value judgments for living life. His Word in the Bible gives us these things, and the Holy Spirit enlightens us to the meaning and application in our own life.

The Last Barrier is Knocked Down

Jesus says to hang out with Him, huddle up with Him, prepare with Him and find rest in Him. Jesus reminds you not to lose your love for Him while you work hard for Him. As you follow Jesus - His life, His Words, His invitation, and His Spirit – you'll grow closer to God. You'll be prepared for battle and for love. Your soul will be better rested and you will therefore be in tune to God's will for your life.

By following Jesus, you develop a personal relationship with the One you will know forever - the compassionate, grace-filled, forgiving, merciful Way to hope and everlasting life. You'll have time to just delight in the Source of all that is good! Jesus blasts *B.N. Busy* out of the way, opening the path for a truly victorious life.

Now that you have followed your Lead Blocker past all eleven adversaries, you're not only believing, but you're trusting. You're not only trusting, you're growing and maturing into an "all-in" Christian who is staying close to the heart of God.

2nd and goal from the 8-yard line. Your Quarterback drops back to pass. You roll out to the left and receive a short pass. A couple of good blocks are thrown by teammates as you run toward the goal post. The only one who can tackle you now is B.N. Busy. Your Lead Blocker comes just in time to once again throw the key block, giving you easy access to the end zone. Touchdown!

* * *

Huddle questions for Chapter 15 small group discussion are found free online at www.UltimateScoringDrive.com

Part V.
Victory

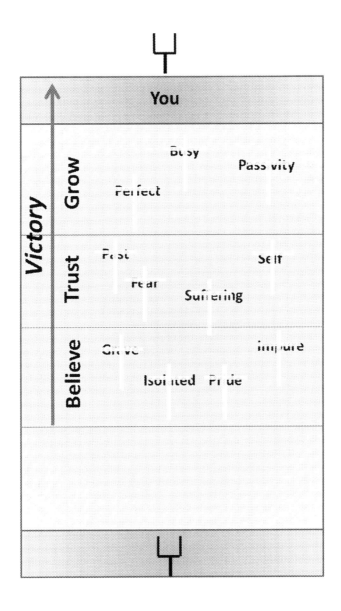

Chapter 16

Victory now and forever

 Upon reaching the end zone you immediately drop to your knees... not for show, but as a humble, sincere and overwhelmingly grateful response to the One who got you there.

Victorious Living on Earth

Thinking back over your drive down the field, you recall the words from your Playbook, "Overwhelming victory is ours through Christ, who loved us" (Romans 8:37b NLT).

Out of love for you, Jesus had come into your life to say, "Come, follow me." When you accepted the invitation and followed:

> ...you came to know God personally and to know that He will never leave you. You followed Him right past *U.R. Isolated*.

> ...you humbly released control to God and allowed Him to work in you and through you. You followed Him to the cross of Calvary where *M.Y. Pride* was leveled.

> ...you saw death defeated and were assured that this life is only the beginning of your relationship with God. You followed Him to His resurrection from the dead where *Barry N. Grave* was conquered.

> ...you were given a bridge over the cliffs of separation that your impure heart and sin created between you and God.

You repented and followed Him to the cross of forgiveness and reconciliation where *Cliff Impure* was nailed.

...life's difficulties, pains and tragedy did not stop your drive. You knew that the Lord understood your pain - He experienced it. You knew He cared greatly about what you were going through. You followed Jesus and knew He was with you through it all. He even made something good come out of the bad. You followed Him right over B*en Suffering.*

...you were led away from faith-distracting, joy-sucking fears, worries, and insecurities. You followed Jesus, and *Max Fear* lost his grip on you, and you headed downfield toward trust, peace, and hope in God.

...your empty life of seeking happiness from earthly self-gratification was exchanged for a life of loving God and others. You followed Jesus into a truly meaningful, significant, joyful, and other-centered life – a life where *M.T. Self* had a much harder time tackling you.

...your anger and embitterment stemming from past hurts was exchanged for a forgiving heart. You followed Him directly past *Red Past.*

...you were freed from a disillusioning and draining belief that God only wants perfection. You followed Him to where there was freedom from being consumed by your own performance. You followed Him around *Noah U. Perfect.*

...you were lifted out of complacency and moved into action – an intentional life of leading your family and sacrificing for God and others. You followed Him and saw *Rusty Passivity* cleared out of the way.

...your soul was at peace and close to the heartbeat of God, delighting in the Lord, and listening to Him and His Word. You followed Jesus into a real huddle with God and found rest away from the noise of *B.N. Busy.*

Overwhelming victory resulted when you followed Jesus. And in the process you met your every core need as a man.

You didn't deserve victory... you didn't earn victory. God's grace carried you down the field. He gave you victory. God drafted you. He called you to play on His team. The Holy Spirit directed you on the field. Jesus led the way. You just followed His lead. God did all the work. As long as you followed right behind Jesus, all you had to do was put one foot in front of the other. All you can say is, "I came on the field to play... I played... I messed up many times. But I followed the One who could take me down the field toward the light of heaven." Jesus led you past the enemy and into victory.

During the scoring drive, your heart was transformed by the Holy Spirit more and more into the likeness of Jesus... overflowing with thankfulness, hope and love that touched the souls of others. You reached out in compassion to others, showing love and respect even to strangers and enemies.

But you know full-well that this heart transformation was far from perfect. In fact, at times the way you lived out your faith felt downright dismal. Setbacks and tough times came your way... doubts, worries, pride and impure thoughts. Heavy blows were dished out repeatedly by the opposition. You had periods when the lens was back on yourself; periods when you were so busy that your relationship with God slid backwards; times when you were in the faith desert; and periods when you were passive about going where God was calling you.

You got tackled again and again. Yet Jesus kept lowering his hand to help you back to your feet. Rising up again, you recommitted to follow Him. Despite your failures, at the gateway to heaven God only sees the righteousness of Christ in every one of Jesus' followers.

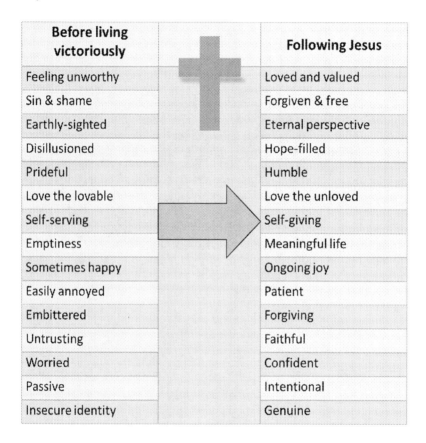

Before living victoriously	Following Jesus
Feeling unworthy	Loved and valued
Sin & shame	Forgiven & free
Earthly-sighted	Eternal perspective
Disillusioned	Hope-filled
Prideful	Humble
Love the lovable	Love the unloved
Self-serving	Self-giving
Emptiness	Meaningful life
Sometimes happy	Ongoing joy
Easily annoyed	Patient
Embittered	Forgiving
Untrusting	Faithful
Worried	Confident
Passive	Intentional
Insecure identity	Genuine

An Eternal Victory

The Bible says that through Jesus, death is swallowed up in victory.

> "For when the trumpet sounds, those who have died will be raised to live forever. And we who are living will also be transformed. For our dying bodies must be transformed into bodies that will never die; our mortal

bodies must be transformed into immortal bodies. Then, when our dying bodies have been transformed into bodies that will never die, this Scripture will be fulfilled:

'Death is swallowed up in victory.
O death, where is your victory?
O death, where is your sting?'

For sin is the sting that results in death, and the law gives sin its power. But thank God! He gives us victory over sin and death through our Lord Jesus Christ" (1 Corinthians 15: 52b-57 NLT).

Following Jesus means you are never separated from the love of God; not on earth and not in the afterlife. Jesus said, "I am the resurrection and the life. Anyone who believes in me will live, even after dying. Everyone who lives by believing in me will never die" (John 11:25-26a NLT). Jesus is going to hold on tight to His followers and keep them with Him on judgment day, after the game is over. Jesus will ensure that your soul will not enter the hell He refers to so often (over 30 times) and that the Bible emphasizes repeatedly (over 160 times). Instead He will save you for an eternity in paradise with Him.

The joy of reaching heaven will surpass anything you experienced on earth. The crowd in heaven goes wild! Loved ones who have gone before you are ecstatic. They know the sweetness of eternal victory and they are so happy for you!

The elation of winning a Super Bowl pales in comparison to the indescribable joy of reaching heaven. Drew Brees recalled the euphoria immediately after winning the Super Bowl. With jubilant fans dancing all around, He and his teammates hugged each other, and were "jumping up and down with joy." [124] Elation was written all over their faces. The players hugged and kissed their wives and children as confetti poured down like rain. Victorious living in the afterlife will be supremely better than this; making an NFL Super Bowl victory seem by comparison like winning a backyard scratch game of football.

When you reach heaven, each teammate comes to greet you. Your Lead Blocker and Quarterback give you a big hug. The Followers Team Leader embraces you with the words, "Well done good and faithful servant."

Before long, you find out that your afterlife in heaven is not a meaningless and boring float trip forever on clouds while listening to harps. You are assigned new responsibilities and duties... important work... yet free of futility and weariness.

All that's promised in the Bible about heaven becomes real in the end zone afterlife. You enter a holy paradise of magnificent beauty, great joy, and immense satisfaction. A place filled with God, with Christ, and with saints and angels. Purity and righteousness abound, with no decay, no corruption and no sin. You're free from hunger, thirst, tears, and fears. There is no death, no mourning, and no pain. Other souls rejoice with you, joining together in fellowship and worshipping God.

One part of heaven is prepared just for you. You enter that room and God commends you for your self-giving sacrificial acts of compassion to others during your scoring drive.

You stand back and smile. Your soul was ready. God had prepared you for heaven. You were prepared through the varied experiences on the field that drew you closer to Jesus. You sought to understand God's truth so that your heart might respond to it and your life conform to it. Your soul trusted and followed Jesus... it was ready to be with God... ready to be trusted with more.

After a time of soaking in the marvelous light of heaven, it's time to get to work... in the universe, doing what God now trusts you to do. That makes you smile some more. Life is good. Eternal life is the ultimate.

Thank you Lord Jesus for clearing the way and leading us into eternity with the Father, Son and Holy Spirit, and with all of God's children. Amen.

Citations and Sources

1   Oher, Michael, and Don Yaeger. 2011. *I Beat the Odds – from homelessness to the Blind Side and beyond.* Gotham Books. New York, NY. 246 pp. Copyright © 2011 - quote used by permission of publisher – all rights reserved.

2   Wood, Gail. 2004. *The Future is Now.* <u>Sports Spectrum Magazine</u>. Jan/Feb 2004. Quote used by permission of publisher – all rights reserved.

3   Wood, Gail. 2004. *The Future is Now.* <u>Sports Spectrum Magazine</u>. Jan/Feb 2004. Quote used with publisher permission – all rights reserved.

4   Brees, Drew and Chris Fabry. 2010. *Coming Back Stronger – Unleashing the hidden power of adversity.* Tyndale House Publishers, inc. Carol Stream, Illinois. 303 pp. Copyright © 2010 - quote used by permission of publisher – all rights reserved.

5   Oher, Michael, and Don Yaeger. 2011. *I Beat the Odds – from homelessness to the Blind Side and beyond.* Gotham Books. New York, NY. 246 pp. Copyright © 2011 - quote used by permission of publisher – all rights reserved.

6   Rice, Jerry and Brian Curtis. 2007. *Go long! My journey beyond the game and the fame.* Ballantine Books, New York. 154 pages. Copyright © 2007 - quote used by permission of publisher – all rights reserved.

7   Smith, Emmitt. 2011. *Game On: Find your purpose – pursue your dream.* Tyndale House Publishers, Inc.. Carol Stream, Illinois. 280 pp. Copyright © 2011 - quote used by permission of publisher – all rights reserved.

8   Weber, Rick. 2004. *The Life.* <u>Sports Spectrum Magazine</u>. September/October 2004. Quote used with publisher permission – all rights reserved.

9   Based on words from Sports Illustrated.cnn.com <u>http://sportsillustrated.cnn.com/danpatrick/blog/125241/index.html</u>

10   Brees, Drew and Chris Fabry. 2010. *Coming Back Stronger – Unleashing the hidden power of adversity.* Tyndale House Publishers, inc. Carol Stream, Illinois. 303 pp. Copyright © 2010 - quote used by permission of publisher – all rights reserved.

11   CBS "60 Minutes" interview of Tom Brady by Steve Kroft. December 2007. Paraphrased.

[12] Sanders, Deion and Jim Nelson. 1999. *Power, Money & Sex: How Success Almost Ruined my life.* Word Publishers. 208 pp. Copyright © 1999 - quote used by permission of publisher – all rights reserved.

[13] Branon, Dave and Paul Johnson. 2001. <u>Sports Spectrum Magazine</u>. Jan/Feb 2001. Quote used with publisher permission – all rights reserved.

[14] Sanders, Deion and Jim Nelson. 1999. *Power, Money & Sex: How Success Almost Ruined my life.* Word Publishers. 208 pp. Copyright © 1999 - quote used by permission of publisher – all rights reserved.

[15] Branon, Dave and Paul Johnson. 2001. <u>Sports Spectrum Magazine</u>. Jan/Feb 2001. Quote used with publisher permission – all rights reserved.

[16] Cooley, Joshua. 2012. *Lead Man.* <u>Sports Spectrum Magazine</u>. Winter 2012. p 87. Quote used with publisher permission – all rights reserved.

[17] Wisniewski, Steve. 2001. *Straight Talk.* <u>Sports Spectrum Magazine</u>. Nov/Dec 2001. Quote used with publisher permission – all rights reserved.

[18] Graham, Billy. 1976. *Day by Day with Billy Graham.* Compiled and edited by Joan Winmill Brown. Billy Graham Evangelistic Association. May 21 devotion.

[19] Dungy, Tony and Nathan Whitaker. 2007. *Quiet Strength.* Tyndale House Publisher, Inc.. Carol Stream, Illinois. 303 pp. Copyright © 2007 - quote used by permission of publisher – all rights reserved.

[20] Brigance, O.J. 2013. *Strength of a Champion: Finding Faith and Fortitude Through Adversity.* The Penguin Group. New York. Copyright © 2013 - quote used by permission of publisher – all rights reserved.

[21] Brigance, O.J. 2013. *Strength of a Champion: Finding Faith and Fortitude Through Adversity.* The Penguin Group. New York. Copyright © 2013 - quote used by permission of publisher – all rights reserved.

[22] Sanders, Deion and Jim Nelson. 1999. *Power, Money & Sex: How Success Almost Ruined my life.* Thomas Nelson. Nashville. 208 pp. Copyright © 1999 - quote used by permission of publisher – all rights reserved.

[23] Dorsett, Tony and Harvey Frommer. 1989. *Running Tough. Memoirs of a football maverick.* Doubleday. NY. NY.. Paraphrased.

24 Alexander, Shaun and Joe Hilley. 2010. *The Walk – Clear Direction and Spiritual Power for your Life.* WaterBrook Press. Colorado Springs, CO. 228 pp. Copyright © 2010 - quote used by permission of publisher – all rights reserved.

25 Smith, Emmitt. 2011. *Game On: Find your purpose – pursue your dream.* Tyndale House Publishers, Inc.. Carol Stream, Illinois. 280 pp. Copyright © 2011 - quote used by permission of publisher – all rights reserved.

26 Weber, Stu. 1997. *Four Pillars of a Man's Heart.* Multnomah Books. Colorado Springs, CO. 286 pp. Copyright © 1997 - quote used by permission of publisher – all rights reserved.

27 Weber, Stu. 1997. *Four Pillars of a Man's Heart.* Multnomah Books. Colorado Springs, CO. 286 pp. Copyright © 1997 - quote used by permission of publisher – all rights reserved.

28 Montana, Joe and Richard Weiner. 1997. *Joe Montana's Art and Magic of Quarterbacking.* Henry Holt and Company, New York. 212 pp. Paraphrased.

29 Sanders, Barry, and Mark McCormick. 2003. *Barry Sanders – Now You See Him…* Emmis Books. Cincinnati, OH. 144 pp.

30 Dorsett, Tony and Harvey Frommer. 1989. *Running Tough. Memoirs of a football maverick.* Doubleday. NY. NY.

31 Morley, Patrick. 1997. *The Man in the Mirror – Solving the 24 Problems Men Face.* Zondervan. Grand Rapids, MI. 379 pp. Copyright © 1997 - quote used by permission of publisher – all rights reserved.

32 Crosby, Jim. 2001. *Super Boulware*. Sports Spectrum Magazine. Sep/Oct 2001. Quote used with publisher permission – all rights reserved.

33 Weiler, Randy. 2002. *Many Happy Returns*. Sports Spectrum Magazine. Jan/Feb 2002. Quote used with publisher permission – all rights reserved.

34 Weber, Stu. 1997. *Four Pillars of a Man's Heart.* Multnomah Books. Colorado Springs, CO. 286 pp. Copyright © 1997 - quote used by permission of publisher – all rights reserved.

35 Warren, Rick. 2002. *The Purpose Driven Life – What on Earth am I Here For?* Zondervan. Grand Rapids, MI. Copyright © 2002 - quote used by permission of publisher – all rights reserved.

36 Tozer, A.W. 1982. *The Pursuit of God.* Tyndale House Publishers. Wheaton, IL. 128 pp.. Copyright © 1982 - quote used by permission of publisher – all rights reserved.

37 Sayers, Gale and Al Silverman. 2001. *I am Third.* Penguin Books. London. 272 pp.

[38] Singletary, Mike and Jerry B. Jenkins. 1991. *Singletary on Singletary.* Thomas Nelson Publishers. Nashville. 220 pp.

[39] Sports Spectrum Magazine. Vol. 27. No. 1. Page 34. Quote used with publisher permission – all rights reserved.

[40] Acee, Kevin. 2005. *Positive Yardage.* Sports Spectrum Magazine. September/October 2005. Quote used with publisher permission – all rights reserved.

[41] Acee, Kevin. 2008. *Better Than Ever.* Sports Spectrum Magazine. Jan/Feb 2008. Quote used with publisher permission – all rights reserved.

[42] Shepatin, Matthew. 2009. *"Then Madden Said to Summerall..." The Best NFL Stories Ever Told.* Triumph Books. Chicago, Illinois. www.triumphbooks.com.

[43] Keller, W. Philip. 1979. *A gardener looks at the fruits of the spirit.* Originally published by W. Publishing Group. Quote used by permission of current publisher Thomas Nelson, Nashville – all rights reserved.

[44] Jenkins, Sally. 2010. *The Coach that Still Matters 40 years After His Death.* Washington Post. Sept. 7, 2010. http://www.washingtonpost.com/wp-dyn/content/article/2010/09/06/AR2010090603019.html

[45] Warren, Rick. 2002. *The Purpose Driven Life – What on Earth am I Here For?* Zondervan. Grand Rapids, MI. Copyright © 2002 - quote used by permission of publisher – all rights reserved.

[46] Tebow, Tim (with Nathan Whitaker). *Through My Eyes.* 2011. HarperCollins Publishers, Inc.. New York. 257 pp.

[47] Wood, Gail. 2004. *The Future is Now.* Sports Spectrum Magazine. Jan/Feb 2004. Quote used with publisher permission – all rights reserved.

[48] Eichelberger, Curtis. 2012. *Men of Sunday – How faith guides the players, coaches and wives of the NFL.* Thomas Nelson. Nashville. 216 pp. (Page 95). Copyright © 2012. Quote used with publisher permission – all rights reserved.

[49] Eichelberger, Curtis. 2012. *Men of Sunday – How faith guides the players, coaches and wives of the NFL.* Thomas Nelson. Nashville. 216 pp. (page 97). Copyright © 2012. Quote used with publisher permission – all rights reserved.

[50] Dungy, Tony and Nathan Whitaker. 2007. *Quiet Strength.* Tyndale House Publisher, Inc.. Carol Stream, Illinois. 303 pp.

[51] Kouki, Gregory. 2005. *Is the New Testament Text Reliable.* Stand to Reason. http://www.str.org/site/News2?page=NewsArticle&id=6068 viewed 7/12/2012.

52 Wikipedia.org. *Biblical Manuscript.* Last modified Feb. 6, 2014.

53 Alexander, Shaun and Joe Hilley. 2010. *The Walk – Clear Direction and Spiritual Power for your Life.* WaterBrook Press. Colorado Springs, CO. 228 pp. Quote used with publisher permission – all rights reserved.

54 Sanders, Deion and Jim Nelson. 1999. *Power, Money & Sex: How Success Almost Ruined my life.* Thomas Nelson Publishers. Nashville. 208 pp. Copyright © 1999 - quote used by permission of publisher – all rights reserved.

55 Robbins, Roxanne. 2001. *No Respect.* Sports Spectrum Magazine September / October 2001. Quote used with publisher permission – all rights reserved.

56 Vick, Michael, Brett Honeycutt and Stephen Copeland. 2012. Michael Vick: Finally Free – An Autobiography. Worthy Publishing. 285 pp. Paraphrased.

57 Rice, Jerry and Brian Curtis. 2007. *Go long! My journey beyond the game and the fame.* Ballantine Books, New York. 154 pages. Copyright © 2007 - quote used by permission of publisher – all rights reserved.

58 Shepatin, Matthew. 2009. *"Then Madden said to Summerall..." The Best NFL Stories Ever Told.* Triumph Books. Chicago, Illinois.

59 White, Reggie and Steve Hubbard. 1993. *God's Play Book (the Bible's Game Plan for Life).* Thomas Nelson Publishers. Nashville, TN. 189 pp. Copyright © 1993 - quote used by permission of publisher – all rights reserved.

60 Dungy, Tony. 2005. *Straight Talk.* Sports Spectrum Magazine. Jan/Feb 2005. Quote used with publisher permission – all rights reserved.

61 Cunningham, Randall and Tim Willard. 2013. *Lay It Down – how letting go brings out your best.* Worthy Publishing. Brentwood, Tennessee. 207 pp. Copyright © 2013 - quote used by permission of publisher – all rights reserved.

62 Yancey, Phillip. 1988. *Disappointment with God.* Zondervan. Grand Rapids, MI. p. 64. Copyright © 1998 - quote used by permission of publisher – all rights reserved.

63 Spalding, Gregory. 2012. *Tackling Life's Adversities.* Sports Spectrum Magazine. Winter 2012. pp 92-93. Quote used with publisher permission – all rights reserved.

64 Warner, Kurt, and Michael Silver. 2000. *All things Possible: My story of faith, football, and the Miracle Season.* HarperCollins Publishers, Inc. New York. 269 pp.

[65] Cunningham, Randall and Tim Willard. 2013. *Lay It Down – how letting go brings out your best.* Worthy Publishing. Brentwood, Tennessee. 207 pp. Copyright © 2013 - quote used by permission of publisher – all rights reserved.

[66] Eldredge, John. 2001. *Wild at Heart – Discovering the Secrets of a Man's Soul.* Thomas Nelson. Nashville, TN. 240 pp. Copyright © 2001 - quote used by permission of publisher – all rights reserved.

[67] Kassulke, Karl and Ron Pitkin. 1981. *Kassulke – True Story of Minnesota Vikings Star Karl Kassulke & the Accident that Changed His Life – For Good.* Thomas Nelson, Inc., Publishers. Nashville, TN. 222 pp. Copyright © 1981 - quote used by permission of publisher – all rights reserved.

[68] Robbins, Roxanne. 2001. *No Respect.* Sports Spectrum Magazine. Sep/Oct 2001. Quote used with publisher permission – all rights reserved.

[69] Brees, Drew and Chris Fabry. 2010. *Coming Back Stronger – Unleashing the hidden power of adversity.* Tyndale House Publishers, inc. Carol Stream, Illinois. 303 pp. Copyright © 2010 - quote used by permission of publisher – all rights reserved.

[70] White, Reggie and Steve Hubbard. 1993. *God's Play Book (the Bible's Game Plan for Life).* Thomas Nelson Publishers. Nashville, TN. 189 pp. Copyright © 1993 - quote used by permission of publisher – all rights reserved.

[71] Eichelberger, Curtis. 2012. *Men of Sunday: how faith guides the players, coaches and wives of the NFL.* Thomas Nelson. Nashville, TN. 219 pp. Copyright © 2012 - quote used by permission of publisher – all rights reserved.

[72] Cunningham, Randall and Tim Willard. 2013. *Lay It Down – how letting go brings out your best.* Worthy Publishing. Brentwood, Tennessee. 207 pp.. Copyright © 2013 - quote used by permission of publisher – all rights reserved.

[73] Eichelberger, Curtis. 2012. *Men of Sunday: how faith guides the players, coaches and wives of the NFL.* Thomas Nelson. Nashville, TN. 219 pp. Copyright © 2012 - quote used by permission of publisher – all rights reserved.

[74] Alexander, Shaun and Joe Hilley. 2010. *The Walk – Clear Direction and Spiritual Power for your Life.* WaterBrook Press. Colorado Springs, CO. 228 pp. Copyright © 2010 - quote used by permission of WaterBrook Multnomah, an imprint of the Crown Publishing Group, a division of Random House LLC– all rights reserved.

75 Montana, Joe and Richard Weiner. 1997. *Joe Montana's Art and Magic of Quarterbacking.* Henry Holt and Company, New York. 212 pages.

76 Montana, Joe and Richard Weiner. 1997. *Joe Montana's Art and Magic of Quarterbacking.* Henry Holt and Company, New York. 212 pages.

77 Honeycutt, Brett. 2012. *True Identity.* Sports Spectrum Magazine. Winter 2012. p 88. Quote used with publisher permission – all rights reserved.

78 Dungy, Tony and Nathan Whitaker. 2009. *Uncommon: Finding Your Path to Significance.* Tyndale House Publisher, Inc. Carol Stream, Illinois. 260 pp. Copyright © 2009 - quote used by permission of publisher – all rights reserved.

79 Alexander, Shaun and Joe Hilley. 2010. *The Walk – Clear Direction and Spiritual Power for your Life.* WaterBrook Press. 228 pp. Copyright © 2010 - quote used by permission of WaterBrook Multnomah, an imprint of the Crown Publishing Group, a division of Random House LLC– all rights reserved.

80 White, Reggie and Steve Hubbard. 1993. *God's Play Book (the Bible's Game Plan for Life).* Thomas Nelson Publishers. Nashville, TN. 189 pp. Copyright © 1993 - quote used by permission of publisher – all rights reserved.

81 ESPN.com. 2008. *In their own words: Fear on -- and off – the field.* October 30, 2008. http://sports.espn.go.com/nfl/news/story?page=hotread7/talent

82 Ortberg, John. 2002. *The Life You Have Always Wanted – Spiritual Disciplines for Ordinary People.* Zondervan. Grand Rapids, Michigan. 272 pp. Copyright © 2002 - quote used by permission of publisher – all rights reserved.

83 Copeland, Stephen. 2013. *Peace in the Walls.* Sports Spectrum Magazine. Volume 28. No. 1. Quote used with publisher permission – all rights reserved.

84 Dungy, Tony and Nathan Whitaker. 2009. *Uncommon: Finding Your Path to Significance.* Tyndale House Publisher, Inc. Carol Stream, Illinois. 260 pp. P. 159. Copyright © 2009 - quote used by permission of publisher – all rights reserved.

85 Sanders, Deion and Jim Nelson. 1999. *Power, Money & Sex: How Success Almost Ruined My Life.* Thomas Nelson. Nashville. 208 pp. Copyright © 1999 - quote used by permission of publisher – all rights reserved.

86 Kassulke, Karl and Ron Pitkin. 1981. *Kassulke – True Story of Minnesota Vikings Star Karl Kassulke & the Accident that Changed His Life – For Good.* Thomas Nelson, Inc., Publishers. Nashville, TN. 222 pp. Copyright © 1981 - quote used by permission of publisher – all rights reserved.

87 Cunningham, Randall and Tim Willard. 2013. *Lay It Down – how letting go brings out your best.* Worthy Publishing. Brentwood, Tennessee. 207 pp. (pages 53 and 175). Copyright © 2013 - quote used by permission of publisher – all rights reserved.

88 Warren, Rick. 2002. *The Purpose Driven Life – What on Earth am I Here For?* Zondervan. Grand Rapids, MI. Copyright © 2002 - quote used by permission of publisher – all rights reserved.

89 Sanders, Barry, and Mark McCormick. 2003. *Barry Sanders – Now You See Him...* Emmis Books. Cincinnati, OH. 144 pp. www.emmisbooks.com.

90 Eichelberger, Curtis. 2012. *Men of Sunday: how faith guides the players, coaches and wives of the NFL.* Page 197. Thomas Nelson. Nashville, TN. 219 pp. Copyright © 2012 - quote used by permission of publisher – all rights reserved.

91 Cunningham, Randall and Tim Willard. 2013. *Lay It Down – how letting go brings out your best.* Worthy Publishing. Brentwood, Tennessee. 207 pp. Copyright © 2013 - quote used by permission of publisher – all rights reserved.

92 Payton, Walter and Don Yaeger. 2000. *Never Die Easy - The Autobiography of Walter Payton.* Villard Books. New York, NY. 288 pp. Copyright © 2000 - quote used by permission of publisher – all rights reserved.

93 Campbell, Bill. 2002. *Double Coverage.* Sports Spectrum Magazine. Sept/Oct 2002. Quote used with publisher permission – all rights reserved.

94 Weiler, Randy. 2002. *Many Happy Returns.* Sports Spectrum Magazine. Jan/Feb 2002. Quote used with publisher permission – all rights reserved.

95 Payton, Walter and Don Yaeger. 2000. *Never Die Easy - The Autobiography of Walter Payton.* Villard Books. New York, NY. 288 pp. Copyright © 2000 - quote used by permission of publisher – all rights reserved.

96 Acee, Kevin. 2008. *Better Than Ever.* Sports Spectrum Magazine. Jan/Feb 2008. Quote used with publisher permission – all rights reserved.

[97] Acee, Kevin. 2008. *Better Than Ever.* Sports Spectrum Magazine. Jan/Feb 2008. Quote used with publisher permission – all rights reserved.

[98] Warner, Kurt, and Michael Silver. 2000. *All things Possible: My story of faith, football, and the Miracle Season.* HarperCollins Publishers, Inc.. New York, NY. 269 pp.

[99] Sanders, Barry, and Mark McCormick. 2003. *Barry Sanders – Now You See Him...* Emmis Books. Cincinnati, OH. 144 pp. www.emmisbooks.com.

[100] Sampson, Jenna. 2009. *Out of the Shadows.* Sports Spectrum Magazine. Winter 2009. Quote used with publisher permission – all rights reserved.

[101] Alexander, Shaun and Joe Hilley. 2010. *The Walk – Clear Direction and Spiritual Power for your Life.* WaterBrook Press. Colorado Springs, CO. 228 pp. Copyright © 2010 - quote used by permission of WaterBrook Multnomah, an imprint of the Crown Publishing Group, a division of Random House LLC– all rights reserved.

[102] Copeland, Stephen. *Unexpected Platform.* Sports Spectrum Magazine. Vol. 29 No. 1.

[103] Chrissy Carew. 2010. *Saints Benjamin Watson.* The Insightful Player. Written March 30, 2010. From website on 1-4-2014: http://www.theinsightfulplayer.com/2010/03/30/benjamin-watson/

[104] Kassulke, Karl and Ron Pitkin. 1981. *Kassulke – True Story of Minnesota Vikings Star Karl Kassulke & the Accident that Changed His Life – For Good.* Thomas Nelson, Inc., Publishers. Nashville, TN. 222 pp. Copyright © 1981 - quote used by permission of publisher – all rights reserved.

[105] Warner, Kurt and Brenda Warner (with Jennifer Schuchmann). 2009. *First Things First: Rules of Being a Warner.* Tyndale House Publishers, Inc. Carol Stream, Illinois. 278 pp. Copyright © 2009 - quote used by permission of publisher – all rights reserved.

[106] Singletary, Mike and Jerry B. Jenkins. 1991. *Singletary on Singletary.* Thomas Nelson Publishers. Nashville. 220 pp. Paraphrased.

[107] Farrar, Steve. 1995. *Finishing Strong – Going the Distance for Your Family.* Multnomah Publishers, Inc. Sisters, OR. 222 pp.. Copyright © 1995 - quote used by permission of publisher – all rights reserved.

[108] Campbell, William. 2003. *Full Speed Ahead.* Sports Spectrum Magazine. Sep/Oct 2003. Quote used with publisher permission – all rights reserved.

109   Jenkins, Sally. 2010. *The Coach That Still Matters 40 Years After His Death.* The Washington Post. September 7, 2010. Washingtonpost.com

110   Smith, Emmitt. 2011. *Game On: Find your purpose – pursue your dream.* Tyndale House Publishers, Inc.. Carol Stream, Illinois. 280 pp. Copyright © 2011 - quote used by permission of publisher – all rights reserved.

111   Burson, Scott. 2006. *Top of the Line.* Sports Spectrum Magazine. Nov/Dec 2006. Quote used with publisher permission – all rights reserved.

112   Weber, Stu. 1997. *Four Pillars of a Man's Heart.* Multnomah Books. Colorado Springs, CO. 286 pp. Copyright © 1997 - quote used by permission of publisher – all rights reserved.

113   Cooley, Joshua. 2012. *Lead Man.* Sports Spectrum Magazine. Winter 2012. Quote used with publisher permission – all rights reserved.

114   Smith, Emmitt. 2011. *Game On: Find your purpose – pursue your dream.* Tyndale House Publishers, Inc.. Carol Stream, Illinois. 280 pp. Copyright © 2011 - quote used by permission of publisher – all rights reserved.

115   Alexander, Shaun and Joe Hilley. 2010. *The Walk – Clear Direction and Spiritual Power for your Life.* WaterBrook Press. 228 pp. Copyright © 2010 - quote used by permission of WaterBrook Multnomah, an imprint of the Crown Publishing Group, a division of Random House LLC– all rights reserved.

116   Sports Spectrum Magazine. 2013. Vol. 27, No 1. Page 13. Quote used with publisher permission – all rights reserved.

117   Tozer, A.W. 1982. *The Pursuit of God.* Tyndale House Publishers. Wheaton, IL. 128 pp.. Copyright© 1982 - quote used by permission of publisher – all rights reserved.

118   White, Reggie and Steve Hubbard. 1993. *God's Play Book (the Bible's Game Plan for Life).* Thomas Nelson Publishers. Nashville, TN. 189 pp. Copyright © 1993 - quote used by permission of publisher – all rights reserved.

119   Rice, Jerry and Brian Curtis. 2007. *Go long! My journey beyond the game and the fame.* Ballantine Books, New York. 154 pp. Copyright © 2007 - quote used by permission of publisher – all rights reserved.

120   Payton, Walter and Don Yaeger. 2000. *Never Die Easy - The Autobiography of Walter Payton.* Villard Books. New York, NY. 288

pp. Copyright © 2000 - quote used by permission of publisher – all rights reserved.

[121] Dungy, Tony and Nathan Whitaker. 2007. *Quiet Strength*. Tyndale House Publisher, Inc.. Carol Stream, Illinois. 303 pp. Copyright © 2007 - quote used by permission of publisher – all rights reserved.

[122] Morley, Patrick. 1997. *The Man in the Mirror – Solving the 24 Problems Men Face*. Zondervan. Grand Rapids, MI. 379 pp. Copyright © 1997 - quote used by permission of publisher – all rights reserved.

[123] White, Reggie and Steve Hubbard. 1993. *God's Play Book (the Bible's Game Plan for Life)*. Thomas Nelson Publishers. Nashville, TN. 189 pp. Copyright © 1993 - quote used by permission of publisher – all rights reserved.

[124] Brees, Drew and Chris Fabry. 2010. *Coming Back Stronger – Unleashing the hidden power of adversity*. Tyndale House Publishers, inc. Carol Stream, Illinois. 303 pp. Copyright © 2010 - quote used by permission of publisher – all rights reserved.

.

Printed in the United States
By Bookmasters